NADINE CRENSHAW

SCULLY

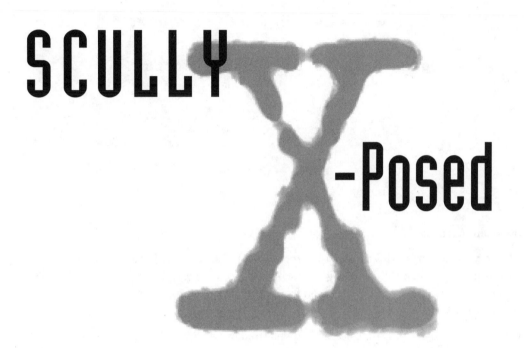

X-Posed

The
UNAUTHORIZED
Biography of
Gillian Anderson
and Her On-Screen
Character

Prima Publishing

D1533782

To my X-Phile son, Rob Crenshaw.

LIBRARY OF CONGRESS CATALOGING-IN-PUBLICATION DATA
Crenshaw, Nadine.
Scully x-posed : the unauthorized biography of Gillian Anderson and her on-screen character.
        p.   cm.
    Includes bibliographical references and index.
    ISBN 0-7615-1111-3
    1. Anderson, Gillian. 2. Actors—United States—Biography. I. Title.
    PN2287.A56C74 1997
    791.45'028'092—dc21   97-19730
    [B]   CIP

97 98 99 00 01 GG 10 9 8 7 6 5 4 3 2 1
Printed in the United States of America

HOW TO ORDER
Single copies may be ordered from Prima Publishing, P.O. Box 1260BK, Rocklin, CA 95677; telephone (916) 632-4400. Quantity discounts are also available. On your letterhead, include information concerning the intended use of the books and the number of books you wish to purchase.

Visit us online at http://www.primapublishing.com

February 24, 1996, Los Angeles, the 2nd Annual Screen Actors Guild Awards. Gillian won the award for Best Actress in a Dramatic Series. Husband Clyde Klotz accompanied her, but their marriage would not survive The X-Files.

G. PACE/SYGMA

May 21, 1996, New York. Fox announced their new fall line-up.
The success of Gillian Anderson and The X-Files *had spawned*
several imitations, such as Dark Skies *and* The Burning Zone.

September 8, 1996, Pasadena, California, the 48th Annual Emmy Awards. Gillian arrived in an Isaac Mizrahi dress. She was nominated for Best Actress, though costar David Duchovny was snubbed by the nominators.

September 30, 1996, New York, the premier of HBO's "If These Walls Could Talk." Gillian's own series, The X-Files, *had recently been moved to a prime Sunday night spot, gathering over one million weekly viewers.*

January 19, 1997, Beverly Hills, the Golden Globe Awards. Gillian and David won awards for Best Actress and Best Actor in a TV Drama. Gillian granted her costar a lingering kiss, tempting fans to believe something was gelling between the pair.

February, 22, 1997, Los Angeles, the 3rd Annual Screen Actors Guild Awards. Gillian was accompanied by X-Files *casting director Randy Stone. Randy backed Chris Carter when he staked his career on casting Gillian as Special Agent Dana Scully.*

You won't admit that you're really
going to be writing what amounts
to fiction. It's going to have
your slant on it—not the truth.
You're just trying to get a handle
on something, a handle on me.

—*David Duchovny to a journalist*

Contents

Preface

EVERY CLUE SUGGESTS THAT GILLIAN ANDERSON is the quintessential private person. As an unauthorized biographer, I have not personally spoken with her. How, then, the reader asks, can I possibly guess who she is? My answer is, How could anyone?

According to the many references and sources I have used, no one outside the small inner circle of Ms. Anderson's life really knows her. I suspect that she mystifies even some of those within the circle. This is part of her magic, the thing that makes her so interesting. She manages, despite her phenomenal fame, to remain ambiguous, a woman of vague outlines, perplexing and paradoxical.

Almost all celebrities sooner or later develop the skill of maintaining their distance from the public who adores them. The rules of stardom were summarized neatly by Esther Williams: "Walk fast. Don't stop and shake hands. You touch them, they don't touch you." Other rules are so common as to be clichés: Avoid any direct glance from a fan. If you must give an autograph, a simple hasty signature will do. Pass through a crowd as if you are indifferent to it and, when possible, while carrying on a conversation with one of your own. If photographers are present, a slight slowing of pace and a careless smile will oblige them. Never, *never* come to a full stop.

Gillian Anderson seems to have been born with a leg up on this knowledge. Though in her business it is necessary to struggle constantly for visibility, maintaining a safe distance seems as basic to her as blinking.

Still, the years of interviews, each containing its own insights, have revealed an astonishing bit of intelligence about my subject, a fragment at a time. I have assembled these bits and pieces to form what I hope is a reasonably true mosaic of Gillian Anderson.

What I see in the pattern is a woman who observes much but reveals little, shows a sensitivity for others, and has a great serenity and reserve, while reveling in life. Although she has called herself a "control-freak," she seems to have no need to dominate others or to willfully invade another's privacy.

Often, such an unimposing disposition causes a person to be overlooked. Not Gillian Anderson. At odds with her desire for privacy is a quirky way of going about living that naturally attracts notice. Her unconventional approach to life is due to the fact that she simply sees different ways of doing things and does them—unaware that they might cause dismay.

Despite her natural reserve and obliviousness to convention, she has somehow succeeded in a profession that is rank with intensity and cutthroat competition and has all the warmth of an intestinal fluke. These paradoxes have made her a darling with fans.

Pictures of her home tell us that Gillian lives a generally relaxed lifestyle. Her activities often seem spontaneous, even scattered. I don't think she planned the tattoo she got in Tahiti or her participation in a long-term television series. She seems to prefer that events just happen. Even important events, like marriage and pregnancy.

I predict that this natural spontaneity will help her to continue excelling in her profession. She inspires an open, diverse environment, creating a fertile ground for the imagination. For that she will be valued by the highly imagination-dependent field of entertainment.

Attuning herself to each day as it unfolds, she seems nevertheless to expect pleasant surprises. I want to believe she will find them.

Chapter One

Dirty, Grungy, and Embittered

ON AUGUST 9, 1968, ROSEMARY ANDERSON, wife of Edward, gave birth to her first child, Gillian Leigh Anderson, in St. Mary's Hospital, Cook County, Chicago, Illinois. The tiny baby's face looked as wrinkled as most newborns'. Soft ash-blond hair framed it. Radiant periwinkle blue eyes gazed benignly at the new parents with unsurprised innocence.

Soon after the baby's arrival, the family moved to Puerto Rico, where they lived for two years. As Gillian grew into a toddler, she displayed a flair for drama that startled her parents. But it wasn't out of sync with her father's interest in things dramatic at that time. From Puerto Rico the family moved to England so that Edward Anderson could study film production at Covent Garden.

Gillian and her family spent the next nine years in London's North End, first in Stamford Hill, and later in Crouch End. She claims few memories of those English years, but photographs exist showing normal family happenings, such as the 1975 vacation in Wales, when Gillian was six years old, and a trip to Ireland when she was seven.

Dreams of becoming a marine biologist developed during a period when she was a tomboy. "I loved digging up worms and cutting them up into little pieces—in the interests of science, of course," she told *Rolling Stone* magazine.

That younger Gillian did not read much, but she wrote several stories. She played by herself or with children in the neighborhood, though she made few close friends. Gillian re-called those years as gray. Of course, London is famous for its gray fogs. Or the period might have seemed "gray" because the family had so little money.

Gillian's parents worked long hours in order to keep Edward in school. Rosemary also took classes and studied computers. They always had several jobs between them. No doubt, young Gillian, often left to her own devices, felt lonely.

Throughout her youth Gillian's bent for drama persisted. Rosemary felt that her daughter had a real flair for the theatrical. It seemed part of the child's personality. During her elementary school days, a teacher wrote one production, called "The Grey Feather," in which Gillian had a part. Another gray thing.

When Gillian turned eleven, however, a change occurred in her life. Edward Anderson couldn't get work in London's film business; the market was depressed. Gillian learned that the family would have to move.

"Gillian was devastated," her mother disclosed to *News of the World*. "We were all sad. We loved London, and hated the idea of moving back to the Midwest."

ANGER BOILS OVER

They returned to the United States and settled in Grand Rapids, Michigan, where Rosemary and Edward still live today. Edward now runs a film postproduction company, and Rosemary is a computer analyst.

That move made Gillian very unhappy. None of the family particularly wanted it. Grand Rapids couldn't compare to London.

Amid the confusion and turmoil of leaving her school and her friends in London, Gillian faced yet another adjustment. Her mother soon gave birth to a second daughter, Zoe. After so many years as an only child, Gillian now had to share her working parents' limited time with a baby sister. Soon, the whole situation would boil over.

Growing up English and then being plopped back down in Middle America as a preteen amounted to no little thing. The contrast was just incredible to Gillian. Grand Rapids seemed a sleepy prairie town under a sky overcrowded with stars. The kids were totally out of it as far as Gillian could see. She missed the sophisticated friends she'd had in London. Meanwhile, the local youngsters snickered at her accent, and Gillian realized she would have to learn to speak "American" in order to fit in at all. (Yet to this day she retains some Britishisms, for instance, calling her mother "mum.")

Even spelling was different. Although American English has dozens of words spelled slightly differently from Great Britain's English, Gillian did extremely well with her schoolwork. Her teachers considered her two years ahead of her classmates.

But Gillian was angry. She felt powerless; and the anger quickly became her way of keeping people at a distance. She acted aloof so that feeling unpopular wouldn't hurt so much. In a *Rolling Stone* interview she talked about the summer before she entered high school, "I wore sweaters and jeans and an olive-drab Army jacket, and it was almost as if I'd trained my body not to sweat." By the time she turned thirteen, she'd started down a path toward becoming a hell-raising teenager.

Rosemary, in the meantime, became pregnant again. Gillian gained a little brother, Aaron.

It was about this time that Gillian joined the nation's punk movement. Although usually reticent in new situations, she soon became a genuine punk rocker, with the nose ring to prove it. She fainted when the ring was inserted into the left side of her nose; and her father went into a fury when he found out.

Gillian didn't cause havoc at home. All during her tough adjustment—accustoming herself to new schools, a new life—she hid her unhappiness

> **❝** She felt her difference from her classmates keenly, and being a punk seemed to make being different an asset. **❞**

from her family. Though she desperately wanted to be in England, her mother claims she never heard Gillian complain.

Her father's disapproval of her nose ring didn't deter her from the path she'd started on, however. She felt her difference from her classmates keenly, and being a punk seemed to make being different an asset. Gillian went on to shave her head, leaving a Mohawk strip that she dyed various colors, changing from day to day. Purple, pink, black. A short person, she stiffened the Mohawk to stand in a plume that made her feel six feet tall. She wore junk-store black clothing and seemed bent on starting her adolescence as the poster model for what seemed a doomed generation.

Her unorthodox appearance and behavior were ways of being in control. She couldn't have been a pretty sight. What is more important, she didn't feel pretty. That assurance wouldn't come, not for years. Yet in shaving her head and garbing herself outlandishly, she gained a sense of having a voice in her identity.

LOST INNOCENCE

During this agitated roller-coaster ride, the thirteen year old lost her virginity to a punk-rock consort. He was no one special, just a boy, another rebel like herself. The experience was clumsy and stupid. "It was not incredibly romantic," Gillian says in Marc Shapiro's unauthorized biography, *The Anderson Files*. "How could it be at thirteen?" It left her with bad memories.

In high school, she drifted off into her own little world—or the principal's office, where she was often sent for talking back. Though bitter to live through, that period in some ways served her adequately. It made her more independent and strong.

To her Grand Rapids City High classmates, Gillian seemed a little alarming. She gave off an aura of being totally self-assured. No one could touch her, no one could hurt her. She was tough. She dressed in black, wore combat boots, and had a hairdo that stood up a foot above the bald sides of her head. The ploy worked on some levels. "But at times, I knew what I was doing was also a crutch," she states in *The Anderson Files*.

Despite her painful first experience with sex, Gillian continued to date—and couple—on a regular basis during her high school years. After forfeiting her innocence, she stepped into a relationship with another punk rocker.

"I was in a relationship with a man ten years older than me when I was fourteen. He was in a punk band, and I used to give him cans of food from our house, and buy him Big Gulps and cigarettes. I was terrible," she told *Movie Line*'s Virginia Campbell.

She knew, even while she remained attached to him, that he lied compulsively. (He would later study entertainment law, which would frighten an older, wiser Gillian.)

That painful relationship seemed just another road sign of the wrong path Gillian had chosen. She accepted it, and dressed and behaved as she did, because she felt dirty, grungy, and embittered. She did not have much respect for herself. Her self loathing manifested in extremes, both physical and temperamental. She sometimes let herself get noticeably overweight, then she would go to the other extreme, becoming acutely thin and unhealthy.

The punk scene in Grand Rapids was predictably small. At first, it consisted of not too many more souls than Gillian and her boyfriend. Then the national punk scene flared up close by in Kalamazoo. Underground bands began to perform there. Gillian saw groups like the Butthole Surfers and the Circle Jerks.

"It was something I needed to do. I don't regret it," Gillian told *TV Guide* magazine. It's not too great a leap to guess that she probably didn't realize how much she needed to express herself artistically.

Some of that need did find expression, however. She painted. Using acrylics, she tried to speak with that something inside her that wanted out.

"In a relationship I was in while I was in high school, my boyfriend called me Gray," she told *Rolling Stone* magazine. Though by then she had descended into a black period. "I just felt I was in the wrong place. I felt like I was in the wrong era. I felt I was in the wrong city." Grand Rapids didn't have enough life for her.

She admits that she brought some of this unhappiness down on herself. She simply couldn't get over her resentment at being moved from a vast world capital to a small city. She felt unbearably restless. She wanted to be creative, but didn't know how to express her feelings. As a result, it was easier to feel dead than to feel helpless.

Gillian's mother glimpsed what might save her daughter. Though Gillian's school work could be better, and though she daydreamed, pulled pranks, and involved herself in a heavy punk scene, an insightful teacher assigned to her the role of Juliet in Shakespeare's famous balcony scene.

Gillian had no background in Shakespeare, and had very little acting practice. Nobody on either side of the Anderson family had any experience with drama. Her father's film production interests were in training films and commercials. But Gillian studied the scene and mastered it without effort. When she performed it for Rosemary, her mother was astounded. Incredibly impressed, Rosemary filed away, then and there, that Gillian would be an actress—*if* she survived the war she seemed bent on fighting against both herself and the rest of the world.

FAMILY TRAGEDY

After Gillian's sixteenth birthday, the family discovered that little three-year-old Aaron had been born with neurofibromatosis, called NF, a rare genetic disorder of the nervous system that causes tumors to form on the nerves anywhere in the body at any time. Gillian's helplessness as she watched her little brother fight this rare disease increased her personal confusion.

"It's been a big part of my parents' and my life," she recounted to *News of the World.* "It's been a major part of my growing up and Aaron's growing up, because of the potential devastation of the disease."

With NF, tumors can grow inside and outside the body. Sometimes the disease deforms—though Gillian objects to that word, preferring "alters appearance." NF can alter appearance severely through large growths on the face and limbs. It is a progressive disorder that affects all races and both sexes, equally. The effects include disfigurement, cancer, hearing loss, vision impairment, epilepsy, bone deformities, and learning disabilities. The tragedy for the Anderson family, and little Aaron in particular, was that NF had no treatment. Tumors could be surgically removed, but they could also grow back.

Gillian began to devote long hours to promoting NF causes with her mother. Rosemary took her to a meeting of what would become the Neurofibromatosis Support Group of West Michigan. A social worker spoke to the forty or so people attending. There were many who felt too intimidated to speak up about their concerns and others who couldn't stop talking, they were so excited about communicating with people who understood what they were enduring. One mother's six-year-old daughter had just died from an NF brain tumor. A sixty-year-old woman tried heroically not to conceal the many disfiguring tumors that covered her face.

Rosemary and Gillian were determined to educate the public about the rare illness. They especially wanted people to understand that it was not contagious. Little Aaron was a normal boy who just happened to have a disorder that could result in brain damage and other difficulties—including death.

> "Acting had a very strange effect on her: it made her feel happy."

Rosemary joined the fledgling support group, and shortly afterward, took over running it with a colleague, Bette Contreras. The group became an instrument of information, education, and emotional support indispensable to NF sufferers and their relatives living in west Michigan. Later, Rosemary helped found an NF clinic near the family home in Michigan.

As much as Gillian loved and sympathized with her little brother, the situation added to her own inner turmoil. A family trip in 1985 back to London, where the Anderson's still owned a flat, did nothing to soothe Gillian's unrest. She maintained her course, seemingly intent on self-demolition.

Late in her teenage years, Gillian reached her adult height of five feet two inches. A petite person, she would later place a cushion on her seat to elevate herself in certain circumstances. Her blue eyes, which had the ability to change, taking on green or gray tints, already contained a steely gaze. Sans her punk makeup, a few freckles dusted her fair complexion. Straight out of the shower, with her remarkable hairstyle wrapped in a towel, she would be considered pretty in a girl-next-door kind of way. A small mole on the left side of her upper lip made an attractive beauty mark. That unmade-up, unguarded Gillian still harbored thoughts of becoming a scientist of some sort, perhaps an archeologist or a marine biologist.

But that possibly philanthropic, possibly pretty, possibly likable girl still seemed headed for trouble. The television series in which she would later star had a motto that could have been hers: Trust no one.

She may have learned, however, to portray many emotions by going through these teenage problems. It helped her grow.

Then, amid perhaps the bleakest moments of her school years, Gillian became involved in the thing that would save her. Acting popped up in her life again when she turned seventeen. She went to several auditions for the Grand Rapids Community Theater, and the director actually cast her in a few things. She never thought about marine biology again. Acting had a very strange effect on her: it made her feel happy. She immediately embraced that feeling. Acting saved her.

Chapter Two

Most Likely to Be Arrested

ACCORDING TO CLASSMATES AT GRAND RAPIDS City High School, Gillian's dramatic skills were evident. She played a demented character in a play called *Zoo Story,* and her performance floored those who knew her only as Gillian the punk, Gillian the rebel. Watching her, they saw another person emerge.

"I have no idea how the transition was made from wanting to be an archeologist or a marine biologist to wanting to be an actress, but it just kind of happened," she is quoted on the "Gillian Anderson Web Site." She felt happy when acting, and that decided her: she'd found her vocation.

The chip on her shoulder began to splinter and fall away. The gray fog began to clear. Her outlook changed, her grades went up, her teachers voted her most-improved student. She began to release some of her pent-up feelings, and started, cautiously, to open herself to the authentic life that existed outside her punk-blinded macrocosm. She began to learn about herself—even found that she held opinions about things.

Ironically, her English upbringing suddenly became an asset. When an English role needed to be filled, Gillian was chosen. After all, she had the accent down pat.

Still, she hesitated to face the world as just Gillian. Exhibiting a facade of rebellion, she finished out her senior year in fine hooligan style. She continued to drink, smoke, and raise hell.

"I was in the principal's office every other day," she conceded on *The Regis and Kathie Lee Show.* She talked in class, stole papers, and threw paper airplanes. Yet her report cards were good enough to ensure she'd graduate.

In her high school yearbook, what caption underlined her picture? Mostly Likely to Appear in a Cult Television Series as the Famous Female Half of an Ultra-hip FBI Investigative Pair Searching the Dark Shadows of Paranormal Activity? "I think I was voted class clown," she informed *TV Guide* with a small smile, "and most likely to be arrested." Her senior year annual shows she was actually voted Most Bizarre and Most Likely to Go Bald.

Despite the fact that she'd begun to find herself through acting, there remained a rebellious fire in her, and in 1986, on the night she received her diploma, the Grand Rapids police arrested her. The charge? Breaking and entering. Later, she would tell Regis and Kathie Lee, "I was a bad girl." Following hours of total excess, Gillian and her fellow revelers broke into City High, and were about to destroy everything in sight, when local police showed up.

The police arrested, cuffed, and chucked a terrified Gillian into jail. Breaking and entering was a felony. If the authorities decided to carry through with an indictment, it would mean big trouble. At least she wasn't eighteen yet and couldn't be held or tried as an adult. Would she be sent to juvenile court, maybe serve time in some reform-school type of camp?

Evidently she refused to give her parents' names, because they weren't informed. Instead, Gillian called her boyfriend to come bail her out. He took his time. She ended up spending hours—almost the entire night—in a cell with drunks, prostitutes, and other common criminals before rescue arrived.

Buried in a suburban Michigan police station may be a poorly lit, cruelly stark mug shot of teenaged Gillian Anderson, nose ring and all. Apparently nothing came of the charges she might have faced. Probably the authorities decided to put it down to graduation night high jinks and let Gillian go, hoping her night in jail would serve as a reminder to behave.

After her eighteenth birthday, in August, she left for college. She hadn't visited the windy city of her birth, Chicago, since returning to the United States, but she had chosen DePaul University as the place to learn more about acting. The Goodman Theater School operated within the university. That would be Gillian's focus for the next four years.

DRAMA STUDIES

Gillian still wore the combat boots and all black attire of her rebellious years. She still talked like a tough punk, though by then she had let her hair grow. And grow. Until it hung long and scraggly. Those who weren't too put off by her crass vocabulary and penchant for slam-dancing found her really quite spontaneous and full of laughter—though even her humor could be raunchy.

> " Those who weren't too put off by her crass vocabulary and penchant for slam-dancing found her really quite spontaneous and full of laughter . . . "

"During college I was somewhat promiscuous," she told Australia's *Rolling Stone.* "But it wasn't fun." She sensed that sex without caring lacked substance.

Her entire curriculum at DePaul revolved around drama studies. She would remember most affectionately the comedy *A Flea in Her Ear,* a farce. Gillian played a small role as a French maid. "It was good for me to explore the comedic side of acting," she said in a CBC (Canadian Broadcast Company) radio interview.

She knew that she was serious sometimes to a fault. Few people knew about her tremendous innate sense of humor. Sometimes she simply cracked up in the most unlikely settings. And when Gillian laughed, everyone laughed. No one could resist her surprising and disarmingly pure sense of outlaw mirth.

Her English accent continued to come in handy for getting parts. She could turn it on and off at will.

While college kept her busy, she managed to continue with her painting, as well. She made herself a home of sorts, furnished with the regulation college-student's futon and decorated with her own acrylics canvases.

She also made a friend who would be around for the long haul. Shawna Franks was drawn to Gillian as a fellow punk rocker at the Goodman School.

SUMMER EMPLOYMENT

One summer while attending school, Gillian ran a restaurant that became very fashionable. It started as a cappuccino bar, then added food to the menu. "And then we started having theater groups in the back. And there was a pool table. And I would make drinks, make food, serve tables, ring the cash register. I mean, I did

everything," she told *Rolling Stone*. She knew she did the work well. And she liked being in control. She called herself "an absolute control freak."

Summers also provided her the opportunity to do bits and pieces with the summer program of the National Theatre of Great Britain, located in Ithaca, New York.

"I was struggling financially and emotionally, and although I had a relatively strong belief in myself, there were times when I questioned my abilities—and my sanity about going into this field," she revealed to Britain's *FHM (For Him Magazine)*.

Sometime during this period, she noticed that nose rings had become common and promptly got rid of her own. She didn't want her personal statement to seem trite.

Also, she gained a film and television credit for a small part in *The Turning*, produced by The Tribeca Film Center.

Chicago began to pall. Even before graduation, she felt primed to get out.

After four years of intensive preparation, she wanted to be in New York City. When her graduating class traveled to Manhattan to perform for an audience of agents, Gillian's monologue impressed someone from the William Morris agency. They wanted to audition her privately.

She went in wearing a vintage dress ten times too big for her, cinched at the waist with a belt. She did her prepared monologue. The agents were impressed enough to say that if she were to move to the city they would represent her, on probation.

Back in Chicago, her heart must have pounded every time she considered the great opportunity she had landed for herself. New York! She set the soonest possible date for departure.

She graduated from DePaul with a bachelor's degree in fine arts. Her parents were proud enough of that B.F.A. to present her with a brand new Volkswagen Rabbit. When the time came for her to take her leave of Chicago, she packed all her belongings, and stuffed the Volkswagen's back seat full. She tied her canvasses and bedding to the top of the compact car. At the last minute, realizing it might rain, she threw a wrapping of plastic over everything and tied it down with a cord.

All this took longer than she expected. At 11:00 P.M. Gillian finally finished. But she had to go, even if she must leave late. "I had it in my mind that I should leave on a certain day, but it took longer to pack than I expected," she told *BC Woman*.

NOW OR NEVER

Gillian absolutely did not want to wake up again in Chicago. So she set out, driving by herself. Indiana, Ohio, Pennsylvania. She drove for hours, stopped for coffee, drove some more. She pulled in behind gas stations to sleep an hour or two in the front seat of the car. "I had to crouch up in a fetal position," she said in a *BC Woman* article. Then she went on driving.

"I couldn't even use the rear view mirror, because of my stuff. I had to use the side mirror," she told *Rolling Stone*. Still a smoker, she kept flicking cigarettes out the Rabbit's open window—until she realized that one of the burning butts might land on her paintings. The acrylics would have made excellent tender. In fact, if they ignited, she wouldn't have time to save her brand new car.

She rolled up the windows, but kept on smoking. The ash tray filled quickly and the car became a moving chamber of smoke.

Gillian finally fell apart in Pennsylvania. Banging her elbow painfully, she realized her body was simply too fatigued to continue. She found a motel called The Castle and crashed, crying herself to sleep on a pillow that smelled like roach spray.

EVERYTHING SHE'D HOPED FOR

New York seemed perfect. Twenty-two years old, Gillian eagerly waited for her career in drama to really begin. "I just felt so alive." The Big Apple had recently redone its streets with little chips of glass mixed in the amalgam, making them sparkle—in Gillian's honor, it seemed.

She auditioned a lot. And worked as a waitress to keep herself afloat. "I worked at Dojo's, on West Eighth. It's like a greasy health food restaurant. Hijiki burgers and stuff like that," she told *Rolling Stone*. It was popular with New Yorkers. Later, people would say to her, "Didn't you serve me once at Dojo's?"

She still wore combat boots, and her long stringy hair was red now—but not a punk crimson-red. Nonetheless, it was a complete mess. "I never combed it. For years," she told *Rolling Stone*.

She also worked at another restaurant that served healthful fare, Village Natural East. More waitress than actress, she grew unhappy. But she did her restaurant work so well that getting jobs posed no problem. In fact, she got them almost too easily.

It seemed to take forever, however, to land the kind of work she'd trained so hard for. In retrospect, she would realize it took only a very short time, but in 1990, youth and impatience made every week seem like a year.

William Morris sent her to auditions for "good stuff"—parts in film features and live theater. "I got two commercials, which never aired. And then I got three jobs in one day," she said to *Rolling Stone*.

But her first big break came from landing a role in an Off-Broadway play by Alan Ayckborne. *Absent Friends* played in the Manhattan Theater Club. Mary Louise Parker originally had the part of Evelyn but she had to back out in order to take a part in the Lawrence Kasdan film *Grand Canyon*. The cast had already rehearsed for three weeks and desperately needed a replacement. Gillian got the job. Everyone recognized her youth and inexperience. They were taking a big risk.

Though she had on occasion withstood "life fright," Gillian suffered an extreme stage fright during her first experience on a New York stage. Waiting for her cue, it felt as if someone had shot

> **". . . Gillian suffered an extreme stage fright during her first experience on a New York stage."**

crystal Methedrine into her arm. The thudding in her heart shook her body and transferred down her arms and legs until her hands and knees trembled spasmodically. She desperately wanted to *get off the stage!* She realized she had lines to say, but her mind went blank.

AUTOPILOT

Then, the long years of training and discipline in anticipation of this moment took over. She began to act—on what she called autopilot. A superb autopilot. Frank Rich wrote in February 24, 1991's *New York Times:*

"... the youngest woman on stage, ... Evelyn, a sullen malcontent with what one antagonist calls a 'really mean little face' and a penchant for speaking solely in contemptuous words of one syllable (usually 'no'). Gillian Anderson, the Chicago actress cast in the part, turns Evelyn into a dark void, a glowering presence as devoid of humanity as [another actor's] Colin is overflowing with it. She is hilarious, if frightening, representative of abject evil."

Gillian received other good reviews, and even won an award from *Theater World* that year.

"And then I ended up waitressing again," Gillian admitted to *Rolling Stone*. Too soon the glory had ended.

Yet people remembered. A man she waited on recognized her, "You were in *Absent Friends*."

"Yes."

"You got all those wonderful reviews. Frank Rich wrote about you, and I read another big *Times* article."

"Yes."

"Well . . . what happened?"

Gillian grew depressed, sad, embarrassed, humiliated.

She did another play, Christopher Hampton's *The Philanthropist*, this time at the Long Wharf Theater in New Haven,

Connecticut. She met someone in the cast and developed a serious relationship.

When the play ended, Gillian went back to New York. He moved out to Los Angeles. When he urged her to visit him, she bought a round-trip airplane ticket, intending a two-week stay.

"I came out to L.A. to visit a man I'd met in a play in New Haven. I was going to stay for two weeks," she told *Movie Line*. But upon arriving in California, "It was like I breathed out for the first time in years." She decided to stay.

She has never revealed more than the first name of the man she had come to visit. *Rolling Stone*'s David Lipsky asked her, "What was the guy's name?"

"I don't want to say."

"You don't want to say?"

"Uh-uh."

But she did reveal that he had established a successful acting career for himself.

"He basically allowed me to be there, to live there with him," she disclosed to *Rolling Stone*.

Gillian moved into his apartment. Later, they rented a house together. He provided most of her support. Although Gillian had some unemployment benefits, she often teetered on the brink of seeking a job as a waitress. But her lover and mentor would say, "No, no, don't. We have some more money. You don't have to work."

She felt incredibly grateful to him for providing her that time. In fact, they were in love. He was in love. Gillian loved him, perhaps but was not "in love" with him.

The William Morris agency had a Hollywood branch. They kept her busy with auditions in her new locale. She rose each day, worked out, tried out for three or four film parts, and then dallied with people met in casting rooms. She felt more relaxed than she'd been in years. The period was really good for her. Everything just seemed to fall into place, at least in a personal way. She hated not having any money and having to rely on her lover to help her financially, but she started to truly open up for the first time and to let people see behind her carefully protected veneer.

She auditioned for everything—including a small role in *Far and Away,* with Tom Cruise and Nicole Kidman, and a couple of director Hal Hartley's films, and *Johnny Suede,* with Brad Pitt. She even "went up" for Sharon Stone's part in *Basic Instinct,* which would later make Gillian laugh at her audacity. After all, she was still showing up for every audition with long scraggly hair, "vintage" dresses, and combat boots.

Those were all the clothes she owned. Although the keen-eyed person might see that underneath this look lived a fashionably small woman with a beautiful smile and large eyes, casting people didn't know what to do with her.

Nor did her agency. Gillian began to feel that William Morris was thinking, We're getting nowhere with this Gillian Anderson; let's get rid of her.

Meanwhile, the California mania for thinness began to have an effect on her. She stopped eating well, and started to become very lean indeed.

> **❝** 'I couldn't put the script down,' Gillian revealed. 'I liked the premise of the show.' **❞**

EXIT TO EDEN

She made a visit to New York, where a friend was pressed for time to make some book tapes for Random House. He asked her if she'd be interested in doing the female voice for *Exit to Eden*, a novel written by Ann Rice (under the pseudonym of Anne Rampling). Gillian jumped at the chance to make some quick money.

It was *very* quick money. The two readers were given just two days to do a read-through of this novel about sadomasochists who find romance amid whips and sodomy. (The novel has little in common with the movie made from it, starring comedian Rosie O'Donnell.) Gillian realized she would have to do several different accents, including Southern and French. There was no time for

research or rehearsal. She simply had to wing it.

Back in California, after being out of work for a year, Gillian began to audition for parts that down-deep she prayed she wouldn't get. "I swore I'd never move to L.A.," she told *BC Woman*, and when she did move there, she swore again that she would never do television. Yet when she landed a guest appearance in the brief TV series *Class of 96*, she took it. The episode was titled "The Accused."

She also auditioned for television soaps, hoping that a break—any break—would come along.

About three months after the *Class of 96* role, a script for a series pilot came to her via her agency. She approached it with doubt. She had no burning interest in science fiction, certainly no driving desire to work in television, and, frankly, her initial introduction to the character of the female lead did not strike a chord of recognition. After all, this Dana Scully seemed insanely intelligent.

The character also had no fear and went into some very dark places. She also remained quite closed to intuition and the paranormal, while Gillian had confidence in both.

Still, the script differed from anything Gillian had thus far read for TV. "I was told it was a good project. It was an intelligent project."

If the character of Scully contradicted the character of Gillian in many ways, at least the FBI special agent behaved in a strong, independent, and thoughtful manner. And it was a leading role. Gillian also liked the intellectual repartee between Dana Scully and the lead male, Fox Mulder. She noted a sexual tension in the first meeting between them, yet the script called for them to contend with each other on a purely rational level. That alone broke all the clichés for male-female TV partnerships.

"I couldn't put the script down," Gillian revealed to *News of the World*. She told *BC Woman*, "I liked the premise of the show. Cover-ups like Watergate and the Iran-Contra affair proved that the American government is quite capable of withholding information from the public 'for its own good.'" Like many of her generation, Gillian believed the government could rationalize that information about visitors from outer space would cause panic, though in other societies around the globe they were accepted as fact. Gillian didn't think the government should decide what people could or could not handle. People had a right to their anxieties, and she'd learned through her own experiences that confronting the anxieties could be quite liberating. Also, if life-forms in other corners of the universe were traveling to Earth, they were obviously more advanced, which meant they had much to teach us. Gillian believed that the population on Earth should embrace that.

Someone named Chris Carter had written the show, which was called *The X-Files*. Gillian decided that she'd like a chance to play this special agent Dana Scully.

Chapter Three

Playing the Deadpan Scully

"I WAS IGNORANT ABOUT TELEVISION. I DIDN'T KNOW what a pilot was, what going to network was, and what auditioning for network was. I didn't know and I didn't care up until then," Gillian told the *Sydney Morning Herald.* Nonetheless, in September of 1993, she auditioned for *The X-Files,* a pilot being produced for the newly formed Fox network. Although as an actress it didn't really matter if she believed in the premise of the story, as a matter of fact, the paranormal had always intrigued her.

"I've always been interested in it," she confessed on CBC's *Real Time.* "It's been something that's been part of my mind and belief systems. [Though] I haven't read a lot of books or subscribed to a lot of magazines."

She arrived at the tryout with her usual dragging hair and black jeans. "It was an audition, like any other audition," she told *Wrapped in Plastic* magazine. She went and did her thing.

She had prepared only cursorily. "I had no idea what the character was supposed to be like, nor did I know what the producers were looking for," she told France's *MAX* magazine. "It wasn't until later that the producers told me that the Fox network executives had wanted a sexy blonde with long legs and [who] looked like a supermodel."

Gillian didn't have those attributes. Not knowing how unsuitable she was, she concerned herself with trying to say the things Dana Scully had to say and trying to sound as if she understood them. Though biology, particularly marine biology, had once engaged Gillian, years had passed since then. At a certain level, Scully lost her. But she had great respect for anyone with that kind of knowledge and ability.

Gillian did well enough to be called back. She met the creator of the series, Hollywood-handsome Chris Carter, and casting director Randy Stone. Arriving in an oversized, borrowed, frumpy-looking suit, she impressed Chris as looking like she needed a meal—which at that time she did. Her eating habits had taken her from thin to skinny.

"When she came in to read for the part, she was not looking her best. She looked like she had probably been living somewhere in the East Village [in New York City] and was dressed kind of funky," Chris told *Rolling Stone*.

Gillian looked nothing like she would just a few months later. But Chris detected an intensity and an intellect there that would be a part of someone who had graduated from medical school, who was alert and ambitious, and who wanted to please her FBI bosses. When he heard her read with David Duchovny,

his choice for the Fox Mulder role, he felt a chemistry between the two actors. Every casting director prayed for that, because it couldn't be manufactured.

Gillian immediately felt Chris's approval of her. She didn't know, however, that he would stake his pilot and his career on her—a risk he would later feel completely justified for taking.

Gillian enjoyed reading with David. His last name, Duchovny (pronounced doo-KUV-nee) is a Russian word meaning spiritual. David often said he didn't care how people pronounced it, so long as they got the meaning right.

Six feet, with brown hair, hazel eyes, and a mole on his right cheek, David was thirty-three years old. A native New Yorker, he had an older brother and a younger sister. The marriage of his father, a publicist, and his mother, an elementary school teacher, had ended when David was eleven. He attended a prestigious private school, Collegiate Prep, in Manhattan, then graduated from Princeton University with a B.A. He went on to earn a master's degree in literature at Yale University, then started his doctoral dissertation, titled, "Magic and Technol-ogy in Contemporary Poetry and Prose."

He wanted to be a writer but equipped himself to teach as a fall-back position. By his own account, he was a tight-assed, repressed student.

While at Yale, he worked as a teaching assistant. He commuted to Manhattan to study acting at The Actor's Studio, as background to possibly taking up screen writing. He soon appeared in a few plays and did a Lowenbrau commercial. In 1987, he left Yale, his doctoral work, and his dreams of writing, to act full time.

David's best known role at the time of the audition for *The X-Files* was the transvestite Dennis/Denise in the TV series *Twin Peaks*. He had a growing list of screen credits, however, including such feature films as *Working Girl, Don't Tell Mom the Babysitter's Dead, Chaplin, Beethoven,* and *Kalifornia.* He'd worked with superstars Melanie Griffin, Harrison Ford, Brad Pitt, and Juliette Lewis.

His work in movies had brought him to the attention of highly placed executives at Twentieth Century Fox, who recommended him to Chris Carter for *The X-Files* pilot.

GOING TO NETWORK

Gillian and David immediately hit it off. David seemed charming and very intelligent to Gillian, who also found him hysterically funny. Though she was actually quite tiny, even frail, as she began to read Dana Scully's part she surprised everyone by coming across as quite formidable.

Gillian learned she was to "go to network" and read for the part again. Speaking to Chris Carter from a pay phone, she got her first inkling of the problems he foresaw in casting her. He told her that she needed to do certain things for the Fox network to gain their approval.

Chris appreciated Fox, which the FCC didn't even consider a real network at the time, for giving him a lot of leeway in creating *The X-Files* pilot. Part of his vision included Gillian playing Dana

> **"** She figured she wouldn't get the part. **"**

Scully. He felt if Gillian would make at least a show of being attractive—such as to dress more appropriately—he could get her the part. On the phone, Chris told her the network would want to see her wear something just a little tighter. And higher heels, please?

Gillian took the middle ground, appearing in a skirt a little better fitting, a little shorter. "In the actual network audition," she told *Wrapped in Plastic,* "there were many, many women left, and David and one other man." They cast David the first day, with Gillian reading with him. But the executives at Fox weren't sure about Gillian. They flew in some more girls. "I had to sit in the hallway with more girls from New York and go in again and read with [David]. It was pretty hair-raising."

She was now aware that they were looking for someone leggier and with a bigger chest. And perhaps with more screen experience. She figured she wouldn't get the part.

Unknown to her, a backroom controversy raged about Scully's part. Chris Carter wanted Gillian Anderson. The executives at Fox shook their heads. They'd acceded to hiring David Duchovny, but to hire two relative unknowns. . . . They panicked at the thought of putting out a show without any star power. Further, they wanted someone with more romantic charisma, more sex appeal.

"It had been proven to them that a particular kind of woman was more lucrative," Gillian said in *Rolling Stone.* She was talking about "T and A," as she called it, two very marketable commodities in the entertainment industry. Later Gillian would joke to *FHM,* "I guess they were going to make this *The XXX-Files.*" Chris

Carter told *US* magazine, "The network wasn't sure how Gillian would look in a bathing suit. They didn't really know what the show was about."

Chris knew he was trying to push a different standard for female characters into the TV world. He understood why the executives were jittery, but at the same time he saw a classic beauty beneath Gillian's gauche facade. He argued that she impressed him as being very independent emotionally, and exceptionally adult and mature. In short, she "played" older than her years. He contended that she had tremendous acting ability and an intensity that would serve the character well. He had a very definite idea about Scully, and he insisted through every argument that Gillian alone had the ability to portray the no-nonsense integrity that Fox Mulder's no-nonsense partner required.

"I stood up in a room full of people and said that I wanted this person and nobody else. I thought later that I'd laid my whole career on the line," Chris told *Producer* magazine.

For a man who spent his time dreaming up conspiracies, Chris Carter seemed surprisingly placid, good-looking, and clean-shaven. He had a habit of pausing to choose just the right words when he talked, as if he were writing his thoughts as he spoke them. The son of a construction worker, he grew up a surfer-boy in a blue-collar Los Angeles suburb. After college, he ambled into *Surfing* magazine, looking for a writing job. Soon he became one of its editors. In 1982, after sitting through *Raiders of the Lost Ark* six times, he recognized his own craving to tell stories. A relative happened to be a talent agent in the film business, and a couple of years later, Chris had a three-picture screenwriting deal with Walt Disney Studios.

He began his career as a screenwriter in 1985. He wrote and produced *The Nanny,* a sitcom for The Disney Channel, and taking a short leave of absence from Disney, he coproduced the second season of the comedy series, *Rags to Riches,* starring Joe Bologna.

In 1992, just as Chris's own dark preoccupations with doubt and government were becoming a national mood, the still-developing Fox network employed him to develop TV shows. "I wrote [the *X-Files* pilot] in my office in my surf trunks, playing with my dog. It never occurred to me that someday there'd be *X-Files* key chains," he told *Entertainment Weekly Online.*

REPRIEVE

Gillian's last unemployment check arrived. She didn't know what to do. Go get a job as a waitress? It seemed the only way, though her lover assured her she didn't need to. Things were looking pretty gray again.

That day, she learned she had won the part of Agent Scully. She felt reprieved—yet surprised. She was no bombshell. It had to be Chris Carter's influence that had won her the part. Once she got over the shock, she whooped for joy. Though she saw television work as a step down, maybe even a sellout, she at least had work.

The series was to be filmed in Vancouver. Casting Gillian had taken so much time that very little remained. Shooting the pilot would already begin later than scheduled. Gillian had to pack and go. But Tim, her lover, suggested they celebrate her good fortune. He took her out to a restaurant, and wined and romanced her.

"Suddenly he asked me to marry him," Gillian recalled for *Here* magazine, "and he presented me with a ring while the waiters and other diners looked on. I should have said no. I didn't want to marry him. But how could I, when everyone was watching me, and willing me to accept? So I said yes."

After that, she hustled straight to West Vancouver, British Columbia, to shoot the pilot.

She barely had time to become better acquainted with David Duchovny as filming began. During their initial rehearsal together, doing the scene in which Scully and Mulder meet for the first time in Fox Mulder's basement FBI office, David played the scene with sarcasm. Gillian came back as if thrown by it, shocked that anybody would speak to her that way. Dana Scully would have reacted in exactly that way. With her strong scientific background, Scully was meant to be a foil to Mulder's wild ideas.

But Gillian couldn't concentrate completely on *The X-Files*. Her mind remained troubled by the stupid thing she'd done back in Los Angeles. She'd lived with Tim for close to a year, and she felt so much gratitude toward him, and owed him so much. But with distance, she felt panicked by what she'd done.

"I realized it was all a mistake," she confessed to *Here* magazine. "It was the first time I'd been away from him and could think clearly." She admitted to herself that she'd agreed to marry a man in order to please some waiters in a restaurant. And to please Tim, too, of course. She loved Tim, but not enough

to marry him. She wasn't right for him. Gillian quickly put an end to all the wedding plans. It hurt them both, but it had to be done, and the sooner the better for everyone.

With that behind her, she returned to her work in *The X-Files* with total concentration.

She assumed that she would shoot the three weeks of the pilot and then return to Los Angeles. People on the set kept talking about being "picked up by the network" and "seasons." She didn't know what the terms meant.

What personal experiences did she call on to play Special Agent/Doctor Dana Scully? Actors can't always rely on personal experience; much of their work is merely pretending. When Scully felt common emotions, such as annoyance or fear, Gillian could depend on her own experiences. But with other feelings, she needed to search further. Scully had a mind that extrapolated. Rather like Sherlock Holmes, she reasoned, deduced, concluded.

> **While filming the pilot, Gillian impressed David Duchovny as a survivor.**

"I'm not that intelligent," Gillian said to *TV Guide*. "I don't have that reference matter in my head. I'm more spontaneous. I laugh." She felt Scully's dialogue frequently sounded very technical. Memorizing it was hard. And even harder to vocalize in an interesting manner.

THE PREMISE

The X-Files posed the premise that paranormal phenomenon—extraterrestrial visits, vampire murders, demonic possessions, and so forth—are regular events. The American government knows about them but refuses to investigate officially, instead keeping the accounts in secret FBI files—the X-files. Special Agent Fox Mulder, who has earned a reputation as a brilliant profiler, gets assigned to looking

into these extraordinary cases. His belief in the paranormal has earned him the nickname Spooky. But certain mysterious persons in powerful positions are nervous about his delving into the X-files. They have Special Agent Dana Scully sent to him, ostensibly to help him, but really to assess his work.

The relationship could be antagonistic; instead, the intuitive Mulder and the skeptical Scully become allies—of a sort. They travel to Oregon to investigate the deaths of several high school classmates. Mulder suspects extraterrestrial intervention, based on such evidence as certain unusual body marks each of the corpses have shared. Scully stands outside the vortex of Mulder's willingness to look for atypical motives—until, after a shower, she finds a mark on her own body. She rushes to Mulder's adjoining motel room and bares her upper torso, asking him to look at the mark on the small of her back. Mulder's pause before he bends to examine the small mark is an example of the restrained "chemistry" that Chris Carter felt between the two actors when casting their roles.

The pilot's subtitle was "The Truth Is Out There." It arrived at no clear conclusion about Fox Mulder's beliefs concerning alien presence, yet strongly inferred that Mulder was right. Dana Scully strived to maintain her scientific skepticism—but given that moment of bared fear, viewers knew that the possibility that Mulder might be right had shaken her.

While filming the pilot, Gillian impressed David Duchovny as a survivor. In one incident, filmed at night, they had to stand in freezing rain. David wanted to call it a night. (In fact, he griped about the Canadian weather a lot.) He noted, however, that Gillian faced the rain machine and actually asked to be hit with more water.

"When we shot the pilot, I was terrified," Gillian revealed to the *Los Angeles Times*. Though she had studied her pro-

fession for years and worked on the New York stage to award-winning praise, she had absolutely no familiarity with television and film acting customs.

"I didn't know what I was doing. I didn't know what 'hitting the mark' was. I didn't know those structures. I learned, slowly."

The executives at Fox watched the *X-Files* pilot in late May, after Chris Carter and his technical team had completed the post-production work. It screened successfully—no, wonderfully. Even top people in the company, such as Rupert Murdoch and chairman Lucie Salhany, voiced their approval. *The X-Files* definitely made the fall schedule.

Gillian was pleased . . . sort of. She really hadn't foreseen that it would succeed and be scheduled for a series. She hadn't taken this television work seriously enough to have any expectations for it.

"I didn't expect it to fail and I didn't expect it to be successful," she told Britain's *Esquire*.

The pilot probably would not have done so well ten years earlier. But Chris Carter and the Fox network correctly gauged that in 1993 people were ready for *The X-Files*. Ideas about UFOs, alien visits, and worse, alien abductions, had once been the stuff of tabloid headlines. Then, novelist Whitley Strieber had written a book he professed was absolutely true about his own alien-abduction experiences. *Communion* made even the most reserved reader uncomfortable. Strieber's sober tone made his message all the more frightening. It became a huge bestseller in the 1980s, as did Strieber's follow-up book, *Transformation*. Readers saw an educated, intelligent man struggling with himself, and with a world that didn't believe him and could not help him. That feeling of being absolutely helpless, absolutely exposed, shook many formerly composed and complacent minds.

After that, several wispy concepts coalesced into a social atmosphere that allowed we were not as isolated on our little blue marble of a world as we had thought. Maybe we were being watched, perhaps by angels . . . or by something less benevolent.

Some could form solid intellectual arguments that there had developed a psychological need for *The X-Files*. "It's been a *really hard* one hundred years for everybody. As we're getting close to the end of the millennium, there's a great deal of metaphysical reflection on where we've been and where we're going," Gillian informed Britain's *Esquire*. Also, nothing was safe anymore. Certainly not a person's job, not his home. All the social and psychic safety nets had been taken away. Many people felt betrayed, and with no one and nothing specific to blame, the time was ripe for vague notions of elaborate conspiracies.

Gillian Anderson believed that humankind simply wanted to feel some hope. Of course, *The X-Files* concerned itself more with the paranormal than the spiritual. Yet she thought the curiosity about things otherworldly showed a need for safety, for a sense of power, for a healing of all the hatreds we had developed. That's how she explained the creation and the network acceptance of *The X-Files*.

VANCOUVER

Gillian reluctantly accepted that, for an unknown time, she was fated to portray a woman for whom exorcisms, alien encounters, and near-death experiences were going to be weekly incidents.

The cast and crew toiled through the summer, producing the episodes needed to fill that weekly TV hour allotted to *The X-Files* through the coming year. The executives at Fox continued to make pleased comments about what they were seeing. Still, who knew how well it would play to a prime-time audience? When September arrived and the premiere of the pilot aired, the cast and crew would find out.

The X-Files originally filmed in Vancouver for purely fiscal reasons. It cost less to film in Canada than in Los Angeles.

A cosmopolitan city in southwest British Columbia, near the border of Washington state, Vancouver is a commercial, financial, and industrial center, and a leading Pacific Ocean port. Among its many cultural attractions are art galleries, museums, a planetarium, and theaters for opera, symphony, and drama. Nearby are two universities.

It is also a very wet place. The soggy Vancouver forests would become standard locations for *The X-Files*. As work continued on the series, Chris Carter grew to like the moody, dank atmosphere that the local climate provided for his dark and gloomy series. There would be little globetrotting for the series' cast and crew. The budget wouldn't allow it.

Gillian and her coworkers never visited FBI Headquarters, though she worked regularly on scenes set in a fictional J. Edgar Hoover building.

Gillian Anderson, one of the city's newest residents, soon learned to keep rain gear handy at all times. The silver lining in Vancouver's infamous rain clouds is the fact that frequent downpours and mists keep the surroundings cleaner and greener than most other cities of similar size. Summers have pleasant temperatures in the seventies; winter days average in the forties.

While all this work went on in Canada, the Fox network scheduled *The X-Files* to air on Friday nights. Some concern wafted through the set about this. Fridays had long been cult night for hardened TV fans. Remember *Beauty and the Beast*? Yet since the end of the *Dallas* and *Miami Vice* boom days, Friday had generated more misses than hits. Chris Carter and his company, Ten-Thirteen Productions, devoted themselves to delivering a reliable lightning-bolt of graphically entertaining terror to those who did tune in. Chris infected everyone on the set with his desire to tell satisfying, smart stories rooted in speculative science. They all set about doing the scariest, most ingenious show possible.

"I had a job, and somebody wanted me to act, and I was happy with that," Gillian told "CBC Midday" radio listeners. But she knew that show business was mostly a business of failure. Out of a thousand ideas, one might be made into a pilot. Out of a hundred pilots, one might make it to series status. Out of ten series, one might become a hit.

An ominous portent appeared before the pilot aired. In its roundup of new fall shows, *Entertainment Weekly* said of *The X-Files*, "This show's a goner."

On Friday, September 10, 1993, America had a chance to judge for itself. The show had been heavily promoted, but so had every other premiering pilot. It began with Julliard-trained Mark Snow's thematic composition on the Synclavier, a decidedly eerie New Age sound that set the mood with precision.

And the pilot did . . . okay.

EXHAUSTION AND DOUBT

"The first year was the hardest in terms of getting into the grueling hours and sleep deprivation and having to perform constantly, day in and day out," Gillian reported on the "Gillian Anderson Web Site." She began to feel like a twilight-zone inhabitant, like the psychics, UFOs, and ghosts that Scully's partner, Mulder, believed in. That unreal feeling included a sense of doubt. Despite her quick success—or perhaps because of it—she questioned her ability. Had it all been just blind luck? Initially, she felt so dubious of her work that whenever the directors and producers clustered together, she feared imminent dismissal.

She also questioned whether she could ever play another character other than Scully.

Playing the deadpan Dana was pretty cut-and-dried, however. Chris Carter had strong ideas about who Mulder and Scully were, and he insisted David and Gillian dramatize the characters' intelligence, seriousness, and motivations as he saw them. Influenced by the success of *The Silence of the Lambs*, Chris wanted Scully modeled closely after Jodie Foster's in-

> **" They all set about doing the scariest, most ingenious show possible. "**

terpretation of that novel-based movie's FBI heroine. Certainly Scully would never overplay the gee-whiz-it's-aliens factor. Further, she equaled Mulder in rank, intelligence, and ability. Chris didn't want her to take a backseat.

In the long run, it's the actor who plays a role, however, and personal flavorings will come out. Yet Gillian and Chris had basically similar ideas about Scully anyway. She settled into a rhythm—with Scully, with the show's mood, with the writing of the character. And since she felt exhausted half the time, she maintained the low-key pattern easily.

Gillian thought she would like Scully should she run into her at a party, but would they have anything to talk about? Scully was not very spontaneous; Gillian was. Other differences were obvious, as well: Scully displayed an enormous intelligence, and Gillian did not; Scully stood five feet six, Gillian did not; Scully could live without a lover, and Gillian could not.

Yet Scully had a very principled mind-set, an honesty, as well as many other positive, forceful qualities. Gillian would have liked to get better acquainted with Scully's private thoughts. How did she have fun? Who were her friends? The scripts dealt only with the character's working life.

"There are many layers to Scully we haven't seen, but I like her mildness," Gillian told *US*.

In the first episodes of the show particularly, and on through most of that first season, Scully remained a skeptic. The scripts set up the audience to side with Mulder, the believer. Gillian soon tired of playing the obtuse one. "There are times when it's frustrating being the negative energy in a situation," she told *SFX*.

The pilot misled viewers somewhat in posting at the beginning of the show

that the story about to be told was true. Actually, it and the following programs were based only very loosely on authentic information. The writers took crumbs and pieces of scientific facts and formulated them into stories.

The show is a stew of many genres: science fiction, mystery, drama, horror, and police procedural. Each episode serves this up with sophistication and humor, avoiding most of the formulaic conventions.

"Some information is factual, but in order to make an episode playable on television, it's pulled and tugged here and there, to make it entertaining," Gillian said during a CBC broadcast. She explained that the stories were constructed mainly for the enjoyment of television audiences.

Chris Carter, like Gillian and David, downsized his personal life to its essence for the sake of the show. "Chris has his hands on every single aspect of the show," Gillian disclosed to *Rolling Stone*. She said the laid-back surfer was "a controlling maniac," but added that he was a genius, as well. His attention to detail could be seen, for example, in Gillian and David's costuming. Since the FBI was rigid about clothing, Scully and Mulder had to wear establishment attire. Soon viewers chided the show for Scully's dowdy suits. Chris Carter thought that unjust.

"It was from people who, I think, watched too much *Melrose Place*," he told *Rolling Stone*. He thought he dressed Scully very nicely. As a producer, he grasped early that even a character who shopped at Sears should wear Armani for the camera. Performers should *always* appear attractive. So Mulder wore Hugo Boss suits, and Gillian wore very fashionable costumes—though nothing that could be mistaken for a design statement.

The two also wore raincoats—often. The trench-style coats were necessary in the cold and wet of Vancouver, and Gillian appreciated them. If *The X-Files* was slated to become TV's creepiest,

most habit-forming series, it would also be its rainiest.

Gillian told *Rolling Stone* that she and David Duchovny worked very well together. "And we can have a lot of fun." Their closeness engendered wild rumors that they were more than just good friends. Which they were. But it was a very complicated relationship—because of the nature of the showbiz world, and because of the nature of who they were as individuals. There are levels of stress and responsibility that come with being on a weekly one-hour drama. And with being one of two leads. They dealt with those stresses in different ways. Gillian tended to internalize. David externalized.

One other difference didn't bother Gillian at first but would fester in time: She received less than half her costar's salary. In the beginning, she understood. He came with ten features on his credits list and she came with only one small screen-work qualification. Later, however, her feelings would change.

Chapter Four

Mixed Blessing

I F SPECIAL AGENT DANA SCULLY COULD LIVE WITHOUT LOVE, Gillian Anderson could not. She had severed her relationship with Tim in Los Angeles, and she was free to find romance on the set in Vancouver. In September, several months into the filming of *The X-Files*'s season one, she noticed thirty-five-year-old art director Clyde Klotz.

"He wasn't on the pilot, but came on board when we started shooting the series," Gillian reported on *The Regis and Kathie Lee Show*. Gillian got to know him better.

"It wasn't quite love at first sight," she reported to the "Gillian Anderson Web Site." "It was Clyde's smile that first attracted me. He was very quiet, rugged, and cool. But I soon realized he had a lot to say, and that he was a very intelligent man."

He interested her, and she had reason to assume he felt the same about her. The pair went out on a few dates, to feel out their attraction.

"It wasn't bang or anything . . . I didn't faint," Gillian said on *The Regis and Kathie Lee Show*. But the two did feel as if they had known each other forever and had just finally met in person. They began a three-month affair and would eventually become privately engaged. Gillian later said cryptically that the engagement was shorter than a month but longer than a week.

She continued to struggle with the fact that she actually had work on a weekly television series. She told *The Washington Times*, "Once in a while I'll be driving down the street in Canada and think, 'I'm in Canada. How did I get here?'"

She occasionally had to go down to Los Angeles, usually over the weekend. When she did, she rarely attended Hollywood parties. Gillian went strictly on business, always related to *The X-Files*— an album release celebration, meeting with the press, exclusive parties with the producers.

Life in Vancouver, the show's long workday, and its remote-from-Hollywood location contrived to keep her from feeling the impact of jumping from being an unknown to being a TV series' leading lady. The show aired in Canada, as it did in the United States, but the very polite Canadians who recognized her kept their distance. No one ever accosted her.

Really, she didn't get out much, according to *The Washington Times*. "I work and I go home. I work on the scripts. I wake up and come to work. And in between I try to get my bills paid."

Gillian's "mum," Rosemary, now in her fifties, met Clyde Klotz sometime

during this period and evidently approved of her daughter's new love interest. She also approved of *The X-Files*. She felt grateful that the series' creator, Chris Carter, had recognized Gillian as perfect for the part. Clearly special from the very beginning, the show represented just the break her talented daughter needed.

When Gillian did begin to be identified, even discreetly, she found it unnerving. "There is something very vulnerable about being in public," she said in an interview with an *Associated Press* reporter. "Having that feeling, hearing 'Scully' whispered as you pass people by. It reminds you constantly that you're not in your private little world."

Meanwhile, she fell deeply in love with Errol Clyde Klotz. One day she invited him into her trailer on the set to eat sushi. Though Gillian's trailer was much larger and plusher than David's, the interior was warm and cozy.

"We were in my kitchen when Clyde asked me to marry him. For some reason the TV was on, showing a couple in bed, and the guy was proposing to the girl.

That's when Clyde popped the question. And I knew it was right," Gillian told *Here* magazine. After a moment of surprise, she found her tongue, and said yes.

They flew to Hawaii during the winter holidays, sending a letter to Gillian's mum and dad with strict instructions not to open it until New Year's Day. When January 1 arrived, Gillian and her fiancé were on the island of Kauai, where they were married on the seventeenth hole of an oceanside golf course. It proved that Gillian retained some of the wacky flair of her earlier years.

They planned a private and somewhat improvised ceremony. They asked the Buddhist monk they'd chosen to perform the rites if he knew of a scenic spot. He suggested the golf club where he had membership privileges.

The site was beautiful, with the blue, blue Pacific stretching into forever and the green dot of the island like a refuge in time. "We kept it very, very small," she disclosed to *The Washington Times*. "In fact, it was just the two of us and a Buddhist priest."

Were her parents disappointed by not being invited? "Mum had already met Clyde, and my dad was in a good mood that day, so they were both happy."

During her brief honeymoon, her imagination, stirred by the material she worked with on *The X-Files*, prodded her to spend some of her time on Hawaii's beautiful beaches looking for "them." For the aliens, the E.B.E.s, the UFOs. Gillian wanted to believe.

PREGNANT

Ironically, *The Star* tabloid reported that during the winter holidays David Duchovny and his new girlfriend, Perry Reeves, had become officially engaged. That was never confirmed, and meanwhile, the tabloid missed the real story.

Gillian returned to work on January third, two days after her wedding, and so did her new husband, both as if nothing had happened. But something had happened, something besides Gillian's change from single woman to married lady. This would soon become apparent, and with it, a storm would descend.

A couple of weeks later, Gillian attended a party in Burbank, given by the Fox network to celebrate the dark, edgy *X-Files* launching. Gillian sat at a table with a woman psychic, Debi Becker, whom Fox had hired to provide a certain paranormal atmosphere and to entertain the party. The woman predicted Gillian would soon give birth.

"I told her I'd just started *The X-Files*, and I could not possibly be expecting," Gillian told *Here* magazine. "But she insisted, 'You're going to have a little girl.'"

That shook Gillian. She had gone to see many psychics over the years and had always been fascinated by extrasensory perception. But this prediction she did *not* want to believe.

Back at work, refusing to accept the psychic's prediction, she worked as hard as ever. For the shooting of one particular scene, she had to fall down repeatedly. By the end of the day, she'd managed to bruise her whole body. Happily, the embryo inside Gillian, as yet unrecognized by her, didn't suffer any consequences.

Within six weeks, however, she felt sick every morning. She had to admit that the psychic was right. She was pregnant.

But Agent Dana Scully wasn't. The cold recognition of that fact trickled down Gillian's back. Her pregnancy would endanger the filming of the show. The situation defined the phrase "mixed blessing." Did the heart-wrenching question of abortion arise? She later told interviewers only that she and Clyde made the decision to go through with the pregnancy.

When Gillian and Clyde were absolutely sure what they wanted to do, Gillian went to David Duchovny. Welcomed into his trailer on the set, she entered and closed the door behind her. The trust between them had grown as the filming dragged on. Taking a deep breath, she told him about her pregnancy.

According to *The Duchovny Files*, by Paul Mitchel, he responded, "Oh my God." He pulled himself together enough to exert some compassion. He asked her how she felt about the pregnancy. Glad, she said.

But what about the show? A very good question, and Gillian had no answers.

Though David must have been deeply distressed, he agreed to keep her confidence until she told the producers.

For several weeks the secret lay between the three—Gillian, Clyde, and David—like an egg about to hatch. Sooner or later, Chris Carter would have to be told the truth.

Some rumors claim Chris went "ballistic" for a while. That would be understandable, considering that he'd convinced the Fox network to trust him with a fantastically expensive show, and then he had pushed them to the wall to accept Gillian as the female lead in it. Not only *The X-Files*, but Chris's reputation, his very career, were all on the line.

TOO PERFECT TO TOSS AWAY

Even with so much to lose, Chris swallowed his unhappiness. He showed sensitivity for Gillian's situation. With one word from him, Gillian would be out, but he backed her decision to continue with the pregnancy.

> **She had gone to see many psychics over the years and had always been fascinated by extrasensory perception.**

Gillian later told *USA Today*, "It was a rough time, letting people know I had made this decision and deciding how to work with it—and for them, [deciding] whether to recast [the role of Scully]."

The producers had to be told next. They were not so sensitive as the two male colleagues in whom Gillian had so far confided. Certain executives saw that the time had arrived to replace Gillian with the kind of femme fatale they'd wanted in the first place.

"It was intense. Everyone was mad at me," said Gillian to *Entertainment Weekly Online*. "It was pretty ballsy of me, after getting such a big break. I was afraid they were going to recast."

The show's ratings at the time weren't sensational. In fact, no one could say if it would last the season. (It finished only as number 102 of the 118 shows in the Nielsen ratings, with a mere 6.4 average.) There were many questions flying around as to what would become of it—and of Gillian Anderson.

On the other hand, there were good portents in the air as well. Viewers for Quality Television acknowledged the show as one of the finest on television. The program also garnered a "Best Drama Series" honor at the Environmental Media Awards. And an Emmy Award for "Best Title Sequence." An Emmy nomination for "Best Music for a Title Sequence." The episode titled "Erlenmeyer Flask" earned a nomination for the Mystery Writers of America's Edgar Award for "Best Episode," and the series as a whole garnered a nomination for "Best Television Series."

Perhaps because of these kudos, which signaled the show might be a sleeper, Chris Carter felt fairly secure. So secure, in fact, that the request from certain Fox Network people to recast Gillian's role took him by surprise. He

has claimed emphatically that they didn't try to *force* him, but whatever degree of pressure they exerted, he refused to give in to it.

Undoubtedly, part of the show's success was the audience's investment in the characters. Chris knew that Gillian played the classic Scully. No one could do the Special Agent like she could. And as for the chemistry between Gillian and David, that was simply too perfect to toss away.

David, too, couldn't imagine anyone else playing Scully. His support meant a lot.

But in the end, it was the fact that the show displayed every sign of becoming a hit that saved Gillian. The Fox network had never had a hit. With just a little blowing on the spark, this *X-Files* series might take off. Sure, the ratings were lousy, but those awards. . . .

And something else was going on. On the world's computers, with the new connection through the Internet, people online gathered to discuss each of the show's episodes, its theories, its stars.

These people apparently adored Gillian Anderson.

The Fox officials acquiesced to Chris's judgment again. But they now added a clause to Gillian's contract—that she couldn't get pregnant again.

Meanwhile, she cut back on the number and intensity of her stunts. No more falling down for a woman in her condition.

Threaded through her personal crises—the proposal, wedding, and pregnancy—was a growing excitement over the fact that *The X-Files*'s otherworldly cases had found a loyal audience, even a small one. Gillian wondered if the show might be more popular if aired on another day of the week.

"Everyone I know who watches it says they tape and watch it on Saturday mornings," she told *The Washington Times*.

Also mixed into the complicated weave of her life was her devoted concern for her brother, Aaron. While stuck in Vancouver, she maintained her close ties with her family in Grand Rapids. Rose-

mary and Ed seemed delighted that their daughter had landed a regular television show. Gillian now had more money than she'd ever made before, which had a good effect on her. She had invariably been generous, even when too poor to give gifts properly. Now she relished being in a position to give lavishly.

FANS AMONG THE FBI

About the time she realized she was pregnant, she became aware of her popularity with groups on the Internet. She took a look once or twice, with people who logged on regularly to "surf" the boards. But what she saw made her decide not to participate often.

"It's very personal stuff, and in terms of the character, I don't want to be influenced too much by people's opinions," she confessed on CBC's *Real Time*. "I have to stick very closely as to how I feel how the character needs to be portrayed from episode to episode."

In an about-face from his original viewpoint, the *Entertainment Weekly* reviewer

> **❝ Within one year, Gillian had gone from being unemployed to starring in a hit series, finding love, getting married, and becoming pregnant. ❞**

much needed break. The first season had proved draining for all concerned, particularly for its leading lady, who had begun to feel pregnant indeed.

Within one year, Gillian had gone from being unemployed to starring in a hit series, finding love, getting married, and becoming pregnant. It was a breathtaking pace. What would the next year of filming *The X-Files* bring?

She told *Movie Line*, "From my perspective, I'm doing what comes up in front of me. I didn't plan for everything to happen in one year. In the moment, these things didn't seem like they were too much."

Now it hit her, however, that it was too much. When the all-too-short summer hiatus in 1994 ended, she went back to the set feeling less able to cope than when she had left it.

The cast accompanied Chris Carter to Washington, D.C., where the creative team of Ten-Thirteen Productions vis-

who had pronounced the show "a goner" now admitted he'd grown addicted to *The X-Files*. He added that the show was the most paranoid, revolutionary thing on TV. *People* magazine's reviewer acknowledged more sedately that if they could keep the mood spooky, the show would have some devoted adherents.

The X-Files and its lead stars were tapping a vein. The demographics people reported that their audience tended to be educated, upscale, and—what proved most important—computer-literate.

Although the first season's standing in the Nielsens wasn't as high as the network would like, Fox renewed the show for another season.

From mid-May to early July, filming of *The X-Files* was suspended for a ited the Federal Bureau of Investigation. Agents swept out of offices and cubicles to meet Gillian and David. Though the bureau had been cautious of the program before, it had seen that the show attracted favorable attention to their work. The good light that *The X-Files* shined on the FBI had increased enrollment at Quantico.

Later, at a Museum of Television and Radio event, Chris Carter spoke about his relationship with the FBI. "When I began working on the idea for the show, I went to [the FBI], and they were very reluctant to give me any information outside of general protocol, but by the end of the first season they had warmed up to us." Agents called and told him they loved the show. And they were beginning to be cooperative, even providing information.

On this trip, however, the feds told the visitors clearly that there were no X-files in actuality and seemed pretty determined that their guests register that fact. Despite the TV program's many fans among the FBI agents—even though J. Edgar Hoover's ghost still haunted the

Washington headquarters—there could certainly be no official connection to the series.

Back on the set, the crew filmed the second season's premier, titled "Little Green Men," scheduled to air September 16. Gillian wasn't working at her normal capacity. She couldn't maintain full energy or concentration in every single scene. It disheartened her not to be on top of every episode.

She was growing heavier each week, as those early-season episodes revealed. She actually gained about fifty-two pounds with her pregnancy. It showed not only in her abdomen, but in her breasts, shoulders, and face. Fans wondered over the Internet if Gillian was gaining weight. The savvy were aware of her pregnancy, while others were in the dark as to the enlargement of her "feminine attributes."

THE CIRCUMSTANCE OF HER CONDITION

Though heavier-faced and heavier-bodied, Gillian still lent FBI Special Agent

Dana Scully that slow-burn blend of gravity and humanity that anchored the witty, dour weirdness of each episode.

If there had been awards for actors who face private challenges without sacrificing professional standards, Gillian would likely be nominated. "My feet were swelling, and I was exhausted, sleeping between scenes," she reported on the "Gillian Anderson Web Site." During her pregnancy, Scully's lab coat and her regulation FBI raincoat came into their own—just the garments to disguise the effects of the developing baby.

"There was a lot of shooting from the neck up, a lot of very high-angles, and a lot of trench coats and baggy lab coats. There was a joke about the cameraman putting on a wide-angle lens," Gillian told a fan during a CBC radio call-in show.

Her hair became so unmanageable it gave her fits. She wanted to shave her head again. Lots of hair spray reined it in, which made it feel even more like an alien *thing* on top her head. She liked hair that got messy and looked real.

The imaginative *X-Files* team worked with Gillian's condition in ways that ranged from the simple to the inspired. Besides the camera angles and baggy clothing, the scripts required less footage of her. When she appeared on screen, Scully mostly sat, or stood behind a concealing autopsy gurney.

Through the practical solving of these problems wove another thread: the show's ratings were increasing. During its second season, it would finish sixty-fourth of 141 shows in the Nielsen ratings, with a 14.5 average.

The show would be picked as "Best Drama of 1994" by *Entertainment Weekly* and get a Golden Globe for "Best Television Drama." Presented by the Hollywood Foreign Press Association, the Golden Globe was significant as a bellwether of popularity.

Furthermore, the American Society of Cinematographers would nominate John Bartley for "Outstanding Achievement." Viewers for Quality Television would nominate *The X-Files* as "Best

Drama," Gillian for "Best Actress," and David for "Best Actor." The Television Critic's Association would soon recommend the show for "Best Drama." Emmy Award nominations would slide in, for "Outstanding Drama Series," "Outstanding Individual Achievement in Writing/ Drama," "Outstanding Sound Editing for a Series," "Outstanding Guest Actress in a Drama," "Outstanding Cinematography in a Series." There would be two nominations for "Outstanding Individual Achievement in Editing/Single Camera Production."

Jeff Jarvis wrote in *TV Guide*, "It's the perfect show for a generation raised on Kennedy conspiracy theories, global paranoia, self-indulgent feel-good cults, tabloids, and talk shows."

The show began to grow beyond cult status and into the mainstream as it achieved its critical mass of popularity. Gillian began to think that perhaps this affair might go on for a good while. She knew they were telling good stories, stories that kept people on the edge of their seats. Also, *The X-Files* looked good because of its high production values (lighting and camera work). Everyone at Ten-Thirteen Productions shared the feeling that they might be entangled in filming for a long time.

That gave Gillian reason to pause—to purse her plump lips. Her feelings were mixed. The show had succeeded; yet it was insane! It meant twelve to sixteen hours a day, five days a week, ten months a year. And she was *so* pregnant.

Chapter Five

Daughter on the Set

A
S IF BOTH CAST AND CREW HAD HEARD THE AWARDS and accolades thundering toward them from over the horizon, an increased confidence glittered on the *X-Files* set during the last weeks of Gillian's pregnancy. Everyone seemed to know they were teaching the field of television drama a lesson in how to uphold excellence week after week. Dealing with Gillian's condition was part of that lesson.

"They don't write scripts until we're just about to shoot them anyway. So they didn't have to do any rewriting," she told *Starlog.* Some scripts had been drafted in less than seventy-two hours.

As Gillian's due date neared, and her pregnancy became too obvious, Chris Carter and his writers developed a plotline in which the X-files investigations were shut down. Scully and Mulder were separated. Scully would be kidnapped, allowing Gillian to remain offscreen for an entire episode.

Those last episodes before the kidnapping episode, however, were pretty rough for Gillian, even though everyone on the set did what they could to accommodate her. As her due date loomed, they filmed the episode in which Duane Barry kidnapped Scully. There were many things that Gillian couldn't do anymore, and that the camera couldn't hide. But they all managed fabulously well with what they had.

The kidnapping led to an abduction by entities unknown. The plot took Scully completely off camera for an entire episode, long enough, everyone hoped, for a ten-day maternity leave. If everything went well, she would have her baby, rest up, and return as good as new. That's what the optimists hoped. In reality, it would be the shortest leave since Pearl Buck's character in *The Good Earth* worked in the fields until her baby began to drop, went inside to give birth, then returned to the fields to finish out the day.

Steve Railsback, known for his career-defining role as madman Charlie Manson in the 1986 *Helter Skelter* miniseries, played an insane-asylum escapee who claimed that aliens were coming for him. Again, savvy fans knew that this first of two parts would set the stage for Gillian's pregnancy leave. As Scully, she would not go gentle into that suspenseful exit, however. She would go screaming, bound and dumped into the trunk of a car.

The last episode in which the pregnant actress appeared was titled "Ascension." In it, Fox Mulder's imagination, fraught with worry over his lost partner, got the best of him. He imagined aliens experimenting on Scully, blowing up her belly like a beach ball. The scene incorporated

Gillian's own nearly full-term bulge, her skin taut and looking exactly as if it were pumped up. Gillian liked that idea.

Chris reacted positively, too. More, he felt that, in the end, the pregnancy had added to *The X-Files* rather than detracted from it, by forcing them all to be so creative.

Meanwhile, on maternity leave, Gillian's due date came and went. Due dates given to mothers are, at best, speculation. The gestating baby decides when it will make its appearance. Gillian didn't have a lot of time in which to lounge about at home, waiting for something to happen. The plan called for her to be written out of the show for one week.

With Gillian out of the picture, debate raged on the Internet as to whether there could be any sexual tension between Fox Mulder and Dana Scully when Scully's alter ego became a mother. How viewers would react to Scully's absence and Gillian's motherhood were concerns at the Fox network. Also, the device that the creative team had used to allow a maternity leave involved some risk. Experience said that a "plot arc"—a plot spanning one or more installments of a weekly series—should not be used so soon in a new show.

Fan reaction seemed positive, however, and ratings climbed. Compared with the first year of filming, the Nielsen ratings for the second season's first eight shows went up 53 percent. In some geographic groups, *The X-Files* rated number one in its time slot.

Fans on the Internet enthused about the baby's upcoming delivery. They sent gifts and made donations to charities in the twenty-six-year-old actress's name. Gillian appreciated the gifts and telephoned some thank-yous by means of an assistant. Even David's fans sent booties and other presents.

TEN DAYS OF MATERNITY LEAVE

Meanwhile, Gillian experienced the passage of time with growing anxiety. Unless

another script was quickly written, keeping Scully out of the story for yet another episode, she had ten days of maternity leave. Period.

She had ten days, then nine, then eight. She felt no contractions, no signs of imminent birth. Her due date came and went. And another day, and another. Two days after her due date, to everyone's great relief, her labor began.

She went through all the trials of a normal labor— perhaps more, because the baby . . . *(push)* . . . would not . . . *(push harder!)* . . . come . . . out.

Surgery became necessary. The doctor leaned over Gillian's white hospital bed, looking from her to Clyde, suggesting a cesarean section.

At last, Piper Anderson (not Klotz), all eight pounds and ten ounces of her, innocent of anything remotely close to crime-busting and science fiction, came into the world on September 25, 1994.

A cesarean section had not been anticipated by anyone, of course. The procedure involves a surgical incision made in the lower part of the mother's abdomen and uterus. Like any operation, it involves risks.

Undergoing major surgery, Gillian was required to spend six days in the hospital. There she received painkillers. She went home with a prescription of Tylenol with codeine, and finished the pills during the next four days.

Then she had to go back to work. She would gladly have stayed home, but she felt something like the crack of a whip above her head: Either she went back or she let the writers hastily insert another episode extending the plot arc of Scully's abduction. "They would have put another episode with me off in space in between," she told *SFX*. That would mean two episodes in which the series—and Agent Mulder—showed they could get along without her. There were still some people who would have liked to see her position on the show undermined, or see Scully recast. She chose to go back.

The producers weren't being calculatedly insensitive to her health. They certainly had their point of view. "The

show was doing well," she admitted on CBC's *Real Time*. "There was a lot of interest in the disappearance, and they wanted to keep the duo [of Mulder and Scully] working together." No one had expected a cesarean section to complicate Gillian's confinement. Given a normal birth procedure, the time originally allotted her, if not exactly generous, should have at least sufficed. Gillian knew that everyone at Ten-Thirteen Productions genuinely regretted the need to bring her back so soon.

The episode titled "One Breath" marked her return. No more could have been done by the writers to make Scully's reappearance any easier for Gillian. In fact, they wrote a script that allowed Scully to lie unconscious for most of the episode.

"I actually fell asleep during the coma scenes," Gillian told *SFX* sheepishly. With sixty people around, and all the lights, however, the situation could not have been completely tranquil. Still slightly blue-faced from the cesarean, she needed very little makeup. David

Duchovny's fine acting also helped to seal Gillian's position. Underplaying the role as usual, he rendered a Fox Mulder so wounded by grief for his partner's apparently impending death that viewers could not help but value Scully as much as he did.

TORN BETWEEN WORK AND MOTHERHOOD

Autumn had by then come to North America. October painted burnt orange and scarlet on each tree. The Friday night "One Breath" aired, a sigh of comfort at Scully's return to the series soughed across the continent. Viewers sat glued to their chairs. Then, as soon as the credits began to roll, those with computers burned up cyberspace. Even Australian fans rejoiced, though the season-two episodes wouldn't be broadcast down under until much later.

It was nice to play being unconscious in "One Breath," but the next episode entailed a return to Agent Scully's old running-and-jumping standards. Though

> **" A sigh of comfort at Scully's return to the series soughed across the continent. "**

Gillian had a stunt double to handle the more physical scenes, the work still challenged her physically. Her frame remained stretched. Bones and muscles were a little off balance, unaligned. Even walking down stairs, her legs could bow out.

The directors continued to make things as easy as possible, but a general exhaustion now followed her. It felt like a huge blessing whenever she could make up for just one lost hour of sleep.

The work now became emotionally draining, as well. Gillian shed an abundance of silent tears. There were times aplenty in the next few weeks that she yearned to quit. Motherhood itself depleted her. "Mostly it's the exhaustion and the stress, but I wouldn't wish it to be any other way in terms of Piper," she reported to *Starlog*. But trying to combine a brand new baby with a fairly new career—and a fairly new marriage—took its toll on her. She wanted to be with her baby. She wanted to bond her family. Instead, she had to work.

The first months of a newborn's life are perhaps the most meaningful time for a mother. Gillian felt a new empathy for working mothers. At least she had Piper nearby. She brought the baby to her trailer on the set and managed to pop in to visit her at every spare moment. But that didn't feel like enough. In her more emotional moments, she really did consider leaving the show.

Gillian certainly would have faced a lawsuit had she made that choice, however. Fox would have had no choice but to sue her for breach of contract. She stayed, and whether she liked it or not, the experience strengthened her.

According to notes circulated on the various computer message boards, even the men pronounced Gillian still as gorgeous and sexy as ever, mother or not. X-Philes everywhere went back to swooning over the resumed erotic tension between Scully and Mulder. "One Breath" showed that the easygoing Mulder cared enough about his scientific-minded partner to want to kill anyone who harmed her.

Gillian's trailer on the set now became a nursery, complete with a nanny. Although the new mother had to work a ridiculous schedule, she felt blessed that *The X-Files* allowed her to have her daughter on the set.

Reaction to the baby by the *X-Files* team seemed positive. Everyone at Ten-Thirteen Productions continued to be incredibly supportive. In fact, Gillian breast-fed her daughter between takes.

Piper created no disturbance during filming sessions. The crew didn't actually see her that much at first. Needing quiet, the nanny kept the baby in Gillian's trailer most of the time.

Yet Gillian continued to feel torn between work and motherhood. A new mother always wants to hover over the miracle she has produced.

At home, Gillian's husband had to learn to cope with his new fatherhood as well. Clyde felt more of a shock at the realities of parenthood than Gillian did. She'd had all the months of pregnancy to prepare. Her body, her mind, and her hormones had had nine months' worth of processing the knowledge of the big change coming. Fathers, Gillian felt, didn't have that readiness—for the sleep deprivation, for instance. But Clyde handled his role very well. He loved Piper to death.

Though her contract didn't allow it, Gillian wanted more children—but not until after the show went off the air. "That's hard, too," she told *BC Woman*, "because the show could run for another five or six years, which means not having another baby for quite a while. But I wouldn't want to do it the same way again. It was one of the hardest things I've ever done."

A DEFINING PERIOD IN HER LIFE

"During the first season, I didn't known who the hell *I* was, let alone who this character was," said Gillian to *TV Guide*. Though she still had not yet grasped her

abruptly gained status as a television idol, she felt stronger in the real world after the baby's arrival. After going through such a difficult birthing process, she felt that no cut, no abrasion, no knock on the head would ever make her whine again.

But despite the ordeal of childbirth, once Gillian had her daughter, she couldn't imagine *not* having her. As she bounced back from the birth with typical buoyancy, she chose Chris Carter to be the infant's godfather.

How did being a mom affect her work? "It's not less important. In terms of time I have to spend on the script, it has decreased. It's frustrating," she said during a CBC broadcast. She put as much energy as she could into the show, yet she said, "I don't take it as seriously as I have taken it in the past. I'm not as obsessed as I was with it before."

The watershed experience of her pregnancy, the birth, and the adjustment to motherhood came to be something of a defining period in Gillian's life. The process of creating a child had grounded her in some way. She had a better hold

> " Her new maturity made her more conscious of her work on the series and the opportunity she had. "

it was sometimes simply inappropriate. But she liked it when it was there.

Her new maturity made her more conscious of her work on the series and the opportunity she had. Looking around the set of *The X-Files* with newly opened eyes, she suddenly very much wanted it to succeed.

She still had little freedom to improvise with the scripts the writers gave her. Anyway, there wasn't time to change it. If it needed to be changed.

Her appreciation of the fine writing for the show became clear when Glen Morgan and James Wong, *The X-Files*'s most popular writing team, departed to produce their own pilot for Fox. Gillian hated that. They were fabulous writers. There were many others out there to take Morgan and Wong's place, but those two writers knew *The X-Files*, and they were good.

Yet *The X-Files* continued to play strongly, even without Morgan and Wong, gaining an ever enlarging following. The

on her characterization of Scully. She felt a new maturity. And with that, she believed she could now do what she'd always yearned to do with her acting.

Her sense of humor went unimpaired by this new maturity. Jesting in an interview with Conan O'Brien, she said of her married name, "Sometimes I go by Anderson-Klotz, or sometimes by Blood-Klotz."

Gillian's friend from her days at DePaul's Goodman Theater School, Shawna Franks, told *US* magazine, "She can be incredibly goofy."

Gillian enjoyed the dry humor in the *X-Files* scripts, though it fluctuated. Writing humor into such a serious format all the time was difficult. Depending on the theme they were handling, series began to generate merchandise sales. Gillian chuckled at the idea of a Scully action figure, and she didn't own an *X-Files* mug. No surprise, since the officially-sanctioned merchandisers had trouble filling orders. Retailers carrying *X-Files* products sold the stuff as fast as it arrived.

Occasionally, the character of Scully loosened up. In the episode "*Excelsius Dei*," for instance, ghosts molested the resident of an old people's home, and the roles of skeptic and believer were reversed between Scully and Mulder. The success of the experiment meant more episodes in which she believed more readily than Mulder.

FAMOUS

On March 4, 1995, the Los Angeles Museum of Television and Radio held its 12th Annual Television Festival, including a special event to honor *The X-Files*. The program had brought television science fiction into the 1990s. Co-executive producer, Bob Goodwin; supervising producer, Howard Gordon; casting director, Rick Millikan; composer, Mark Snow; Chris Carter; David Duchovny; and Gillian Anderson were invited to be praised and questioned. In the audience were Chris's wife, Dori Carter, and David's girlfriend, Perry Reeves.

Gillian came onstage wearing a black jacket, a black gathered skirt, with a black leather backpack slung over her shoulders. A return to her punk-frump days? No; this was Gillian's quirky humor at play. She removed the pack and jacket to uncover a low-cut dress in black-and-white check.

The evening began with a showing of "Duane Barry," the episode that had set up Dana Scully's still unexplained abduction. The episode also included a scene in which Mulder climbed out of a swimming pool wearing a Speedo swimsuit, making it memorable for David's female fans. As Gillian watched the screening, the quality of it verified the fact that every episode of *The X-Files* compared favorably with theatrical films.

During the question-and-answer session, the audience wanted to know about such things as the cast's visit to the FBI, Chris's ultimate idea of the aliens' purpose in hassling the human race, and possible *X-Files* spin-off programs. Humor filled the relaxed evening. A question arose from the audience about the effect of the show on the creative team's beliefs in extraterrestrials. David quipped, "Unfortunately, Gillian and I have been indoors for eighteen hours a day for the last two years, so we've never seen any [aliens]. We assume that you all have seen them while we've been working."

He also joked that he and Gillian were both convinced that Chris was an alien.

One questioner stressed that since Scully's disappearance had been so fantastic, it seemed odd that the character hadn't reflected on it. Gillian answered that often people have episodes in their lives that they don't want to examine. "It may be too much for you to deal with right now, so you wait and you put it off."

Another viewer wanted to know if he would ever see her laugh. Gillian

protested tongue-in-cheek, "We laughed once."

David agreed, saying they were very lighthearted.

Chris added, "If you know Gillian, she's got the greatest laugh. It's the most girlish, easy laugh, and I don't know why it never appears on screen. I think because her character is so serious."

Asked if he intended to do a theatrical *X-Files* film, Chris joked he would—as soon as Jodie Foster and Richard Gere were free.

Viewers said that a few episodes, such as "Beyond the Sea," seemed to hint that Scully had psychic abilities. That had not been Chris's intention. "But you know, my answer to that is, anything can happen."

Howard Gordon joined the discussion to explain that the genre was pretty new, and they were discovering as they went along how to best scare people. It would be all too easy to slip into certain horror conventions and go for the easy scares. The trick was to make the show as believable as possible, so that everything took place within a realm of possibility—extreme possibility perhaps, yet possible nonetheless.

Following a mention of *Star Trek*, Chris quickly said he'd never watched a single episode of the show. (He held private concerns over comparisons between *Star Trek* and *The X-Files* that he did not discuss at this event.)

The X-Files won the Golden Globe Award for "Best Drama TV Series" in 1995, beating out favorites like *NYPD Blue* and *ER*. Ratings for *The X-Files* had nearly doubled since its debut.

Behind the excitement of the Golden Globe ceremony night lurked a small embarrassment for Gillian, something of a humbling nature for one who had risen so quickly. Quentin Tarantino attended the ceremony, and Gillian assumed, judging by the genres he liked, that he would be familiar with *The X-Files*. So she walked up and introduced herself. He shook her hand politely, but she knew he hadn't a clue as to her identity.

Well, all right, she was famous, but not famous enough for Quentin Tarantino to know her yet.

Nevertheless famous enough to be asked to do her very first television talk show with Regis and Kathie Lee.

Chapter Six

Just a Hard-Working Girl

I F   W E   C O N S T R U C T   A   T Y P I C A L   (T H O U G H   F I C T I O N A L)
workday for Gillian, say a Friday in spring of 1995, Gillian wakes to drag herself out of bed in the morning. "I probably get about five hours' sleep a night," she reported to *Starlog.* She often forgoes breakfast, drinking decaffeinated coffee, bottled water, and sometimes a nutritional supplement that looks like a milk shake.

She immediately goes to the Ten-Thirteen Productions studio and puts herself at the mercy of makeup and hairstylists. Any faint reminder of her nose ring is hidden by the thick makeup used for filming. Her hair is no longer done for the show in a style that she feels makes her look like her mother, as in the first season.

While various cosmeticians fuss over her, David Duchovny consults with the show's writers, going over the minutiae of the script with all the concern of a former English teacher. Much of Fox Mulder's drollery is either ad-libbed by David or comes from insider-jokes between him and the writers.

The entire studio, a cavernous place, is very busy, indicative of its stature as a major production center. Each show requires a huge amount of work. Each installment starts with a two-week preparation, followed by eight or more days of the principal shooting, requiring twelve to sixteen hours a day—which means continuing late into the night. And that is just the main photography. The second unit crew spends even more hours on each show.

At any time, there are actually three different installments in the works: primary photography for the newest script; finishing-work on last week's script; and in the offices, duplication of the script for next week that runners then deliver to the heads of each department—hair, makeup, wardrobe, props, set decoration, design, locations, special effects, and construction.

Gillian has a "hand double" in the second unit. This woman fills in for her in almost every shot that doesn't require her face. Thus, Gillian and David can work on scenes that do require her face, and, of course, her special, slightly slurred enunciation. The costars don't get the luxury of continuity. They might film scenes from several different episodes during a single week, and must keep each story and its emotions in mind.

For our simulated typical day, a scene must be filmed first thing this morning for a show Gillian thought they had completed last week. The episode needs to be extended. Chris Carter has written something quickly, just to add a few minutes.

Filming begins. Standing in the middle of his living room, FBI Agent Fox Mulder is absorbed in a conversation with Scully about his lost sister, Samantha, abducted nearly two decades ago by aliens.

Cut. The two deadpan FBI agents become David Duchovny and Gillian Anderson. David turns away, steps past the Panavision camera toward a hall of the studio. He slumps into a canvas chair and takes up a notebook. He writes, possibly working on some of the poetry he struggles to produce at irregular intervals. David misses the live poetry readings in which he used to participate in Los Angeles. His writing talents have led him to supply the outline for two of the show's episodes, "Colony" and "Endgame," both of which aired in February 1995.

The set is a friendly place. Everybody loves working on *The X-Files,* even though it's hardly a picnic. They work double shifts every day, sometimes until two in the morning, often in rain, occasionally even in sleet and snow. Gillian is tired almost all the time. Carrying her half of this hour-long weekly show leaves her few hours for her new family, yet she maintains a positive attitude. And somehow copes.

Another scene is shot. Another break. David kids around with a prop coordinator while Gillian receives a massage from the show's masseuse and tries to focus. Behind a set's fake wall, a production-team member speaks in flat, confidential tones to one of the many reporters always petitioning to be allowed on the set. Anything to do with *The X-Files* makes good copy.

Talking to the reporter, the employee says guardedly that aliens abducted her late last year. They took her up in a spaceship. It was hard to remember, dreamy. They spoke to her telepathically. The only thing she remembers distinctly is that the aliens had three fingers.

Is she putting the reporter on? Perhaps. He writes it all down diligently. It's just the sort of thing he hoped to get, just the thing to spice his article and make it salable to an *X-Files*-hungry public. On a wall nearby

this exchange, the sign above Mulder's desk says, "I want to believe."

GILLIAN HOLDS IT TOGETHER

Gillian, loosened by her massage, must prepare for a stunt. While she works, David walks his pet dog, Blue, who is the daughter of the dog featured in a first-season episode, "Ice." Blue is known on the set as a foot-licker.

An hour later, as the show's production cycle moves on, Gillian sits at a table in the midst of a faux-country kitchen set. She's cleaning a handgun as Mulder leans close, pressing some theory on her doubtful mind. "Mulder," she replies, "the only thing more fortuitous than the emergence of life on this planet is that, through purely random laws of biological evolution, an intelligence as complex as ours ever emanated from it." She speaks flatly, exuding the intimidating, bookish dignity expected from a physician/FBI agent who is also well acquainted with *Webster's Dictionary*. "The very idea of intelligent alien life is not only astronomically improbable, but, at its most basic level, downright anti-Darwinian."

Something about the line tickles her. The corners of her mouth twitch.

Once *TV Guide* asked Mitch Pileggi (who plays Scully and Mulder's boss, Assistant Director Skinner) what about Gillian did he think would most surprise fans. Mitch didn't hesitate: "Her sense of humor. Once she gets the giggles, it's like, forget it."

At the table, Gillian tries to stifle a laugh but a small twitter escapes, becomes a giggle. Then full-fledged laughter.

Once started, she can't stop. She calls it being "slap happy." She drops her head, surrendering to giddiness. David turns aside in his chair, trying not to smile.

Off camera, the crew breaks out in uncontrollable giggles. Gillian's laugh is infectious. She wipes tears from her eyes. The cameraman admits defeat. Cut.

No two personae are more opposite than Gillian and the brainy scientist she portrays. The scenes are always a bit bizarre for that reason—Scully is forbidden any of the natural levity Gillian possesses.

Chris Carter, who loves her effortless laugh, feels she could be a terrific comedic actress—but not on *The X-Files*.

Gillian holds it together, and they get through the scene in the kitchen set. Once it's "a wrap," she hurries back to her trailer to check on Piper.

At four o'clock, the lunch break is called. Gillian warms her lunch in her trailer's microwave while Piper sleeps in the trailer's second room.

Off camera, the alliance between Gillian and David greatly resembles the one they act: They are perfectly congenial, but they also know perfectly well when the other is exhausted and irritable—which David clearly is today. They have great respect for the fine-tightrope walk they do all the time. Gillian admits they have their ups and downs. At times it's difficult; they both tend to be quite moody. But underneath they care about each other. It is this care that comes through in the rapport they enjoy before the cameras.

Preparing for the next scene, David wanders around his character's cluttered office, intended to be in a basement of FBI headquarters. He hardly looks at the paraphernalia Fox Mulder has supposedly collected. Someone out of sight drops something. Colorful vocabulary rings out. The reporter tries to get a few words from David, who is charming one moment and brusque the next. David meanwhile learns there's a problem with shooting the upcoming scene. He has a free hour. He retreats to his spartan trailer. Blue follows at his heels.

From the start, David received more notice in the media than Gillian. She felt that was due to his being in the business longer. Gillian's agent and publicist urged her to remedy the disparity.

IT'S A WRAP

Dana Scully's apartment is one of three standing sets in the cavernous sound stage. Not many scenes are filmed there. The agents are more often on location, chasing unknown answers far away from their fictional base in Washington, D.C.

> **"No two personae are more opposite than Gillian and the brainy scientist she portrays."**

Gillian finds her character's home somewhat alien, though it hardly changes from month to month.

Scully lives "shabby chic," according to a set decorator named Inget. Gillian would be hard-pressed to choose anything from Scully's apartment that she'd want in her own Vancouver home. It's all a little too IKEA for her. She prefers Mulder's apartment and furnishings.

Back to work after breast-feeding Piper, Gillian—or rather, Scully—must give her dog, Queequeg, a bath in the kitchen sink. Between takes, Gillian gasps and waves her hands in front of her face; the dog apparently has a wicked gas problem. Gillian holds her breath while giving her lines. Once it's a wrap, she complains, "Something is dying inside that dog!"

(In a future episode, Queequeg will be suitably punished. The dog will be eaten, presumably by an alligator.)

Somehow, through the long day, Gillian remains serene—as eerily serene as her *X-Files* character. At nine o'clock, she leaves the studio behind and stands in the damp Vancouver night. At least two hundred people—actors, sound and lighting guys, various assistants and hangers-on, as well as several bright-eyed spectators throng the residential street corner during the stop-start filming of a chase scene. Gillian stands on the shiny macadam amid a maze of viperous cables and camera equipment. A neighborhood curfew means the filming will wrap "early" tonight. That means by 11:00 P.M.

"Usually on a Friday night, we'll be shooting until three in the morning," she told *The X-Files Official Magazine.*

Her weary optimism is characteristic. She and the rest of the company spend their lives in a state comprised of battle fatigue, deadline stress, and caffeine-fueled hyperactivity. Gillian gives her co-workers enormous credit. "I wouldn't be able to do this without their support and generosity and sensitivity," she told the magazine.

After the interminable hours on the set, she goes home. At least tomorrow is Saturday, and she doesn't have to learn pages of dialog tonight for the next day's filming.

Her social life is extremely restricted. She and Clyde don't get out much at all. She shoots *The X-Files* five days a week, and weekends are now family time.

Gillian and David rarely socialize together, because they already see more of each other than anyone else in their lives.

SOME JIGGLY, STAPLE-THROUGH-THE-NAVEL STARLET

The same spring as our fictional day, Gillian did get away from *The X-Files* long enough to do an installment of *The Simpsons.* (The episode wouldn't be aired for nearly two years, because it took the producers more than their normal six months to develop it.) In the program, Homer spots a UFO, and Scully and Mulder try to help him figure out what it's all about. Gillian loved *The Simpsons*, and she felt it was the ultimate accolade to be on it. To her, it showed she'd really arrived—that and being in *Mad* magazine.

Mad called her manager's car phone while Gillian was with her. They put the proposal on the speaker phone. Such offers could still thrill Gillian.

Playboy also called—not "Heff" himself, though apparently he loved the show. It was an invitation to a party at Hugh Heffner's house. Apparently the magazine wanted to feature her—her large and mesmerizing eyes; her red, full mouth; her . . . other physical endowments. They offered her money. How much?

"A lot. But I turned them down," she told *FHM*. She had no desire to be flung into the public mind as some jiggly, staple-through-the-navel starlet. "But it was very flattering, I must say."

One episode of the series struck Gillian as particularly fun. She grinned

as she recounted to *SFX*, "In 'Humbug,' we move into a town that's full of circus freaks." Jim Rose's circus worked with them. "It was bizarre. One man hammers a nail into his nose on screen, and someone else ate a live fish." The script called for Scully to eat a bug. The crew had prepared, at considerable expense, several chocolate bugs just for her. However, when she saw that another performer had to let live insects crawl all over him, even out of his mouth, she felt ashamed. After all, was she an actress or a prima donna? She ate a real bug herself. But she didn't swallow it. She spit it out as soon as the director called, "Cut."

Fox network executives felt extremely pleased with *The X-Files* as the second season wound down. They contracted for another three seasons, which in turn meant a substantial elevation in salary for Gillian.

Still not as elevated as David's, however.

When the annual hiatus from shooting finally came, Gillian gave up her va-

> **Gillian's sexuality was cerebral, and therefore far more potent.**

cation, or what the British called her "holiday," to do a different kind of work—promotional touring. The Fox network whisked her around Europe. Talking to Britain's *SFX* magazine, she tried to assure the reporter that Agent Scully was just a hard-working girl and not sexy at all. The reporter in turn informed her that in the country where she had spent her early childhood, she was called the Thinking Man's Crumpet.

"'Thinking man's crumpet?'" she said. "Well it's more flattering than being a lobotomized man's crumpet, I suppose."

It was in praise of her real-woman look, which did not conform to prevailing television beauty standards. She didn't have the mile-long legs and the mammoth breasts, or a tiny nose and matching intellect. In short, she did not display a mere caricature of sensuality. Gillian's sexuality was cerebral, and therefore far more potent. Great Britain's press insisted that underneath her character's sensible suits and anally styled 1940s hair there lived a fiercely sexual id.

She didn't grasp what any of that meant, what people were raving about, why the fuss. A sex symbol? Gillian couldn't see it. She certainly didn't *feel* like a sex symbol.

But then, again to *SFX*, "Somebody asked me the other day what it was like working with a sex god like David Duchovny, and I can't get that out of my head. Sex god?"

ONE PETAL

Though *The X-Files*'s second season had made Gillian a woman known throughout sixty countries, she still barely thought of herself as a star. The leap to seeing herself as a fantasy object seemed just too incredible.

She hadn't had the time to analyze what the program's success and her own role in it meant. Gillian shrugged all that off; a professional concentrated only on the quality of her work. She refused to consider this stardom people said she had, let alone an *international* stardom.

Male devotees of *The X-Files* appreciated her attractiveness, however. They knew that some actresses, whatever their role, are aware of their beauty, while Gillian didn't seem aware of it at all.

An extra on one show had done a fortune-telling trick behind the scenes by drawing a triangle, a square, and a dot. She told Gillian to pencil in a picture around each of the shapes. Gillian drew one petal and several leaves around the dot. The woman said that the leaves, being green, represented growth, and that the single petal revealed that Gillian perceived herself as not in full flower.

Gillian had not prized herself in the recent past. She'd spent time being overweight, underweight, wearing black, hiding behind makeup and hair dyes.

She told *Movie Line*, "In the past couple of years, I've started to open up. What's scary is that I'm doing it in front of millions of people."

She did it so well that people all over the world were struck with admiration, but that hadn't really sunk in yet. Her twelve- to sixteen-hour days, five days a week, ten months a year had insulated her. And there she was, spending her vacation working on *The X-Files* as well.

She did take the time to drive through her old neighborhood, Crouch End, during her visit to Great Britain. But she didn't stop. It was "pissing" rain, she said as any native Londoner might. She slipped back into her old accent as easily as into a warm bath.

Many of Gillian's favorite performers were British—Gary Oldman, Ralph Fiennes, Emma Thompson. The idea of one of them making an *X-Files* appearance, however, horrified her. Well, it would be fabulous if Gary Oldman could step into the show for just a day (certain stars had shown interest in doing guest spots), but it would distract too much from the program. It might take the viewers away from the environment—the mood—that Gillian et al. needed to maintain.

Her various interviews across Europe suggested that the mood had got its talons into Gillian. She had no problems accepting the more bizarre phenomena depicted in the show. Why not? She had been intrigued by the supernatural since childhood. She would love to see some real aliens. It seemed so probable that something "intelligent" other than earthlings existed in this universe that she didn't doubt it for a minute. Government concealment wouldn't surprise her, either. Concealment was synonymous with government.

That sense of having reached maturity with Piper's birth continued to make her feel strong—someone who had something to offer. The questions she'd had about her talents during the first two years of filming *The X-Files* were dissolving.

It was a successful working vacation, yet busy and tiring. And what Gillian really needed more than publicity was sleep. To get a few days of that before filming recommenced, she returned to Vancouver and the snow-tipped British Columbian mountains that formed such a theatrical skyline beyond the city.

Chapter Seven

Best Lead Actress

B Y NOW GILLIAN HAD RESIDENCES IN BOTH LOS ANGELES and Vancouver, but she felt more at home in the Canadian city. She was learning to cope with working and living there, though it had been difficult in the beginning. According to *TV Guide*, she called Vancouver "a small town." But her new husband was a Canadian citizen, and Piper had dual citizenship, so Gillian felt she would probably never leave Vancouver completely. Her family would be going back and forth, even after the show concluded—whatever year that might be.

Both her homes were considerably more glamorous than her trailer on the set, which was comparable to a motel room with a sofa, shag rug, and glossy wooden table. It was thin-walled and movable.

Gillian acquired a puppy, a black Italian mastiff, that quickly grew into a sizable dog. She named it Cleo. The animal stayed indoors more than David Duchovny's Blue. She seemed to know that the most relaxed place to be on a set was in a star's trailer.

Inside her private space, Gillian often wore a baseball cap and prescription glasses. She looked like any young woman, pretty yet real— someone you might know. Her personality was easygoing and bubbly. Yet when she spoke, Scully's voice came out—and Scully's laugh and Scully's way of nipping some sounds and drawing out others. Fans as well as professional journalists inevitably found that fascinating.

Actors may not be their roles, yet they plug into their characters their own voice and movements. It charms, but can confuse people who don't know them well.

As Agent Scully, Gillian was known from Tel Aviv to Tokyo, from Lisbon to L.A. And she soon might be a bona fide movie star. When Chris Carter started seriously talking about making an *X-Files* feature-length film, Gillian was dismayed.

"It just seems like a . . ." she floundered during a CBC interview, "it's hugely ambitious for the schedules that we're all working under right now. It sounds wonderful, but I'm . . . you know . . . I also question the value of, um, having a feature come out while the show is still running."

She argued that it might be better to wait to do a feature-length film when the series was no longer running anymore, when fans didn't have a new episode to tune into every week at home.

Surely part of her hesitation concerned the conflicts she already had between her schedule and her desire to spend more time with her husband and daughter. One Friday night when Gillian wasn't at home, Piper's nanny reported that the baby recognized her mother on TV. She toddled up to the set to get Gillian's attention. The scene ended, and the baby cried. She couldn't understand where her mommy had gone. Just the kind of incident that could break a working mother's heart.

A DEFINITE ATTITUDE

That autumn of 1995, Gillian agreed to do a risqué photo shoot for *FHM*. The idea was to feminize Gillian. It was a conscious effort to broaden the public's perception of her, to ensure that a restrained—FBI agent image didn't cling like cold treacle for the rest of her career. It might also get her some of the widespread attention that David Duchovny was already getting in such large doses. The ploy would have echoes she didn't anticipate.

She was slated to do her first appearance on *The Late Show with David Letterman* in November, but the program was postponed until February.

"Maybe that was actually a good thing, because I'm actually nervous about doing *Letterman*," she observed philosophically to a *Los Angeles Times* reporter. In a late-morning interview in a Sunset Strip restaurant, she said, "Maybe I was meant to have a longer period of privacy."

Yet she knew that none of David Duchovny's three appearances on the show had been postponed. She tried to believe there was a cosmic answer to why she hadn't received the widespread recognition he'd got. She needed to think there was a reason for it not happening to her yet—or maybe not happening at all.

Gillian tried not to feel that she and David were in competition. She graciously admitted that David could slip into various situations and be absolutely engaging, while she wasn't like that. If she walked into a party too full of agents, producers, and the like, she felt awkward. And she would leave. She refused to schmooze.

But Gillian was settling into her role and beginning to take stock of her new life, which was completely different from the one she'd had such a short while before.

"There were steps in the process that were hugely frustrating, and I felt like I couldn't talk to anybody about it, because nobody could really understand," she told *Flair Online*. She'd got through those stages, however, and she accepted the changes.

Chris Carter continued to maintain that Gillian was actually quite like Scully. But the truth was, the more comfortable Gillian got with the character she played, the more Scully became like Gillian. Sometimes Scully looked up at Mulder with a definite attitude that was pure Gillian Anderson.

Though Scully remained the strong, doubtful yin to Mulder's gnostic yang—showing none of Gillian's quirky and charming sense of humor—her skepticism was not shared by the actress. Gillian had always been fascinated with certain paranormal phenomena like ESP and psychokinesis. She believed in UFOs. In that respect, she and Scully were very different.

However, Chris was right about Gillian's tendency to be as single-minded and as obsessed with her work as Dana was. Glen Morgan referred to Gillian as "very smart," and Chris was impressed by how hardworking she was. Chris had not forgotten her willingness to show up for filming during her pregnancy and after her surgery-assisted delivery.

IMAGE

Reporters had come to know Gillian as a more difficult interview than either Chris or David Duchovny. *Rolling Stone*'s David Lipsky recounted, "At times our talk felt chatty, and at times—particularly when we landed on emotional and family subjects—she would clam up, and it felt like an interrogation." Lipsky added, "Anderson would smile before she repeated, 'I don't want to talk about it. Uh-uh. Not even a little bit.'"

US magazine quoted her as saying, "I have adopted a new policy to not comment whatsoever on my personal life. I just need to do that because stuff has been so misconstrued. I say purple and they print pink, and there's nothing I can do about that."

She's been burned in the press, particularly by the tabloids, and burned by so-called friends as well. She was shocked that three times in the last few years she had trusted friends who later betrayed her confidence.

Gillian was again in Los Angeles in January to make an appearance at a weekend convention of the official *X-Files* Fan Club. And to discuss several movie prospects. She'd decided she couldn't afford to wait until the series ended. Her fame was spreading, and she must not miss any chances.

The X-Files's arduous nine-and-a-half-month shooting calendar still narrowed her choices, however, and she desired to be with her husband and daughter. She told a *Los Angeles Times* reporter, "It's like a death sentence, really." She softened that with, "But you get all the mineral baths, good catered food, flowers, and all that stuff. So it's a good death sentence."

She also said she was praying to God that *The X-Files* wouldn't go on for another four years, even though she was contracted for that many seasons. She felt serious reservations about *The X-Files*'s ability to stay vibrant more than another two or three seasons.

❝ 'I have adopted a new policy to not comment whatsoever on my personal life.' **❞**

"You have to wonder how much longer they can pull off these original scripts. After a while they are going to have to start pulling from old ideas, and everyone's going to be comparing this one to that one." She hoped the producers had sense enough to pull out while the show remained fresh.

The candid, perhaps careless, remarks of that interview would cause her some problems with Chris Carter. He would remind her what an opportunity she had been given. Gillian realized her mistake, though at times her terrific luck must have seemed a little too much of a good thing.

The fan convention was planned for January 13 and 14, in Burbank—the "beautiful downtown Burbank" of Johnny Carson's jeering monologues.

Well, not exactly downtown; more like out near the airport. Gillian was booked to appear on the second day, a Sunday.

According to *Starlog*, fans had complained that the convention center would be too small to hold everyone who wanted to see her. It had only one large ballroom, with a capacity of seventeen hundred. No one at Fox had quite grasped that an entire subculture had formed around the noirish Friday evening drama series, currently rated third-highest for television viewers from eighteen to forty-nine years old. Two years ago, *The X-Files* barely blipped on the ratings radar. But it had come a long way, and far faster than some could keep up with.

The facility was more than suitable for the Saturday crowd, which numbered about six hundred. The event's professional managers felt confident that they had things under control. Videos and slides from the program were projected on the walls, giving the cavernous hall the proper atmosphere. The worst problem seemed to be a situation in which a dealer was making photo ID badges that looked like FBI badges. Network representatives felt it might expose them to legal headaches, so the popular enterprise was shut down.

Fox also ruled that no *Star Trek* products be sold or displayed. Two British University of Northumbria sociologists had recently said 10 percent of *Star Trek* convention attendees were maladjusted and suffering from addiction to the series. Understandably, Fox was guarding its own *X-Files* fan image carefully.

Chris Carter was also concerned about over-merchandising the show. He tried to keep a lid on it, to make sure that anything that went out represented the true spirit of *The X-Files.*

Those restrictions aside, devoted viewers, who called themselves X-Philes, happily spent the hours between 10:00 A.M. and 6:00 P.M. searching out T-shirts, auto-graphs, and most importantly, answers. They gathered in enclaves to discuss the show's chic editing and its attractive stars.

X-PHILES EN MASSE

Sunday dawned, and fans began to show up for Gillian's appearance. As warned, the place filled, and then became jammed. Seventeen hundred attendees—they could let in no more—paid between seventeen and fifty dollars to get into the hall. Merchandizers' tables had to be moved to a distant room in an adjacent hotel.

Gillian waited in the wings of the packed ballroom while a twelve-minute collection of video clips featuring Scully played on a giant screen. Gillian was nervous, according to *Starlog*, yet she knew it would be foolish not to experience this. She told *The Los Angeles Times*, however, "It will be my one and only convention experience."

She was not one for large gatherings, and this seemed a huge affair. And there she was, with nothing to say, really. She had assumed she would go out on the stage and talk briefly: Hi, I'm glad you like the show, thanks for having me here.

Chris Carter had taken the stage at the first convention, in San Diego the preceding June, and admitted he hadn't been prepared for the firing line of flash-bulbs. Though it took him only minutes to recover from his surprise and call up his inner ham, Gillian was much more introverted.

The audience applauded louder after each successive clip, and went wild after the one from the newest *X-Files* episode. When the lights came up, Gillian whipped up the necessary courage. She walked onto the stage—to a thunderous ovation.

More people had been recognizing her in public lately, and the number who approached her had tripled. She'd received loads of devoted mail from all over the world. But none of that had prepared her for X-Philes en masse. According to *Starlog*'s Stephen Walker, her first words were, "Holy Cow."

Gillian found the audience's reaction to her unbelievable. And overwhelming. Why hadn't she prepared a speech? All she could do was ask for questions from the crowd.

Without pause, a throng of fans rushed forward to talk to "Scully." She responded to every question as truthfully as she could, including those that didn't really deserve a response, like: If she were peanut butter, would she prefer to be chunky or smooth?

Doug Hutchinson, who had played the eerie Eugene Tooms on the two most raved about episodes from the first year's *X-Files*, happened to be standing among the fans. He asked Gillian how it felt to have that handsome Tooms actor rolling around on top of her. (Eugene Tooms was a monster who made meals of the raw livers he pulled out of his victims bare-handed.) Gillian didn't at first recognize Doug, who stood back with a sinful glitter in his eye. Gillian said the Tooms actor was really a very nice guy, and only realized Doug's joke when he said, "I'd love to take you out for some liver."

After the Q & A session, Gillian signed autographs—for a line that had grown several blocks long before she'd

> **Gillian laughed at any suggestion of a romance with David.**

even finished speaking. The next three hours were almost as grueling as filming *The X-Files*. She sat at a table scribbling her name until her wrist cramped.

If Fox had underestimated Gillian's popularity before, they would not do so again. Particularly not after the Screen Actors's Guild Awards two months after the fan convention. Clyde accompanied her to the 1996 SAG ceremonies in March. She was honored as "Best Lead Actress in a Drama Series." David was nominated, but didn't win. Later that year *The X-Files* would skim five Emmy's. Other awards poured in. The Directors Guild of America nominated Chris Carter for "Best Director of a Television Drama," for the episode titled "The List." A nomination for "Best Television Drama" came in from the Producers Guild of America. The list went on. And on.

FED FATALE

The work went on. And on.

Once in a while, a really good script dealt with the things that drove Scully and Mulder emotionally and psychologically, and Gillian found those episodes the most provocative. She felt that they made better shows—things like "Beyond the Sea" (first season) and "Irresistible" (second season). Gillian wished there were more of those episodes. They told about the personal lives of the characters and formed a mythological background for the tales. Perhaps running that kind of story consistently would be inappropriate, considering the show's premise. But the audience loved anything hinting of what they termed mythology, and Gillian thought they could do at least a little more of the personal material.

The gossip machine went into overdrive when Gillian and David posed in bed together for steamy publicity pictures that soon showed up on the cover of the Australian *Rolling Stone Rock and Roll Yearbook 1995*. That was the sort of moment fans lived for: their favorite "fed fatale" and her partner *in bed together*. At last.

Starlog reported that, when asked how she liked being so close to David, Gillian showed enough sauciness to clarify the question: "You mean, what was it like having my naked breast against his chest?" After a good laugh, she said, "It was fun, his skin is soft, he was gentle."

Apparently happily wed, Gillian laughed at any suggestion of a romance with David. It was a photo! Merely part of her job, to promote the show. Something thought up and allowed by the costars because the idea sounded like it would make a great cover. If there were anything between them, she claimed, they wouldn't have done the cover at all.

Another photo had Gillian in bed with both David and Chris. "Alien Sex Fiends," the caption read. Still another shot showed Gillian, David, and his dog, Blue, in bed.

Gillian thought the photographs risqué and beautiful. She loved them. The whole idea appealed to her quirky love of the unconventional—which she hadn't been allowed to express for far too long. The real Gillian was breaking out a little.

But that was all it amounted to: A few photos—albeit, scorching ones.

The growing amount of publicity she was doing was matched by the growing momentum in *The X-Files*'s ratings. All the signs indicated that the series wouldn't end for a long time. People were seeing something worth watching on Friday nights. Gillian's interviews with the press began to sound repetitive: She felt that not only was the show timely and the audience ready for it but *The X-Files* was particularly well done.

In truth, the scripts were good, and they steered the characters of Scully and Mulder down some very interesting lanes. Better ratings meant more money from the Fox network. Chris Carter had a full wallet, so each episode looked great. The stars looked great. People loved the entire ambience that wafted through the airways.

The subject matter of the show was perhaps its first attraction to viewers. But Scully's relationship with Mulder was a close second. The platonic professionalism that overlaid the sexual tension between them fascinated everyone, male and female fans alike. Of course, there were still some obtuse viewers who didn't actually sense the subtle sexual tension. Gillian herself had heard from fans who didn't feel any of what the others were going on and on about. Sometimes she wondered if the tension had decreased over time.

Yet the relationship between the characters had developed further during the past year, inevitably changed by everything they had endured together. Scully now had a more open mind. She had evidently seen enough that she was not as quick to think Mulder was wrong anymore. She listened to what he said, and rather than coming from completely converse directions, the pair found the truth together. Scully would never be the believer her partner was, however.

"Scully's as open as she's going to get. She has a need to go back to finding the scientific and plausible solution behind stuff. So that's how she's going to perceive stuff first and foremost," Gillian told *Starlog*.

Making Scully multifaceted within the show's often emotionally dry environment continued to be a challenge because of the character's function: Scully must remain the skeptic, the scientific voice to ground the bizarre happenings. Mulder continued to be the true believer—and thus came across as the more heroic figure.

That was a problem that continued to plague Gillian in her attempts to stay on a par with her charismatic costar.

Chapter Eight

Images

I N APRIL, THE *FHM* ARTICLE AND ACCOMPANYING photographs of Gillian hit the stands in Great Britain. "I remember looking through the issue I was in, and then two pages after me were all these plastic dolls in all these weird sexual positions, and I thought, 'What the f— is this? What have I got myself into?'"

The dolls were Barbie and Action Man posed to show women's favorite positions for sex. The dolls didn't have any genitals, keeping the feature just this side of pornographic.

Yet there was a taint to the article. *FHM*'s reporter called Gillian for a second interview. She told him, "I remember someone saying, 'I was pissing in a toilet and sitting above the toilet was a magazine with you on the cover, and I think it was called FH-something or other.' That was particularly memorable."

With the magazine's publication, however, parts of the planet went Gillian Anderson mad. The article that accompanied the lingerie-style photos told how she lost her virginity at age thirteen to a boy who later became a neo-Nazi. But the main attraction to buyers were the photos of Gillian in various languorous poses, wearing barely-there items of black lingerie.

The copies flew off the racks in record time. Disappointed fans who didn't get hold of a copy began to badger the magazine's offices with beseeching letters, outlandish swap requests, even death threats, in the futile hope of being sent the sold-out edition. One hopeful American even mailed the British publisher an unsolicited check for two hundred dollars.

Though Gillian had posed for the magazine, she seemed ambivalent about the mass media attention. She tried to ignore it, claiming *The X-Files* was the celebrity, not her. Yet magazines with covers featuring David Duchovny, had never done nearly the volume of sales that the *FHM* issue did.

The most entertaining reaction to the sexy photo shoot came from the most unlikely source. Gillian's grandmother wrote to her saying, quite tongue-in-cheek, that she was very sorry Gillian had no clothing left. Maybe she should send Gillian some money to buy a thing or two. The old lady said she planned to plant some fig trees, so there would be plenty of fig leaves if Gillian were to run out of clothing again.

Not only its stars were being made famous by *The X-Files* but Chris Carter's celebrity was growing apace with Gillian and David's. It didn't happen often for a producer-writer to become as famous as

his series. The examples were few; Alfred Hitchcock and Rod Serling come most readily to mind. Once the show started, strangers sought Chris out—regular folks, not the nut cases that might be imagined. A banker told him about an experience with aliens. Flight attendants leaned over his passenger seat and, in low tones, claimed to have observed UFOs.

"One friend told me, 'You don't know how accurate you are.' He broke down, telling me about his visitations," Chris told *Entertainment Online*. "I've known this person for two years. I have no reason not to believe him."

Though other members of the crew reported similar incidents, that was one thing Gillian did not experience. People did not approach her on street corners or in restaurants to tell her about paranormal episodes and wild nightmares. Why would they? After all, she played the skeptic.

On the other hand, she didn't get out that much. When she did, it was usually only to go shopping near her home—

wearing a coat and glasses, trying hard not to resemble the sex symbol in *FHM*.

POTENT EFFECT ON MEN

Gillian's brother, Aaron, turned fifteen. Gillian had watched him grow into a sturdy boy. The Andersons were among the most fortunate of neurofibromatosis families. Aaron was only mildly affected by the disease. So far so good. But with NF, the worry was never over.

In May 1996 Gillian attended a Neurofibromatosis, Inc. luncheon in Washington, D.C. She went with her mother, who was still copresident of the NF Support Group of West Michigan. While there, Gillian delivered a speech encouraging education about NF and funding for NF projects. Present were , Michigan's Senator Abraham; Senator Nancy Kassebaum, chairman of the Senate Labor and Human Resources Committee; Dr. Francis S. Collins, Director of the National Institute of Health's National Center for Human Genome Research; and Dr. Martha Bridge Denckla, director of the developmental cognitive neurology division of the Kennedy-Krieger Institute in Baltimore. Gillian's remarks were entered into the *Congressional Record*.

While in Washington, D.C., Gillian and Rosemary visited the local Fox morning news show, and Gillian taped a public service announcement on neurofibromatosis, which would be broadcast nationally over the Fox network.

According to her speech to the NF, Inc. luncheon, her brother, Aaron, had been lucky so far. Usually the arrival of puberty caused the disease to grow swiftly. However, Aaron had only a couple of visible skin tumors. He might have no more; but he might have so many more they would become uncountable. And there was always the threat of the more serious tumors that interfered with vital internal organs, like the brain. Those could show up at any time. The family lived with fingers crossed.

Aaron had regular medical examinations, though the disease had been relatively uneventful in his case. When

Gillian spoke of him, it was always tenderly. She thought him incredibly bright, athletically skilled, and beautiful. His illness continued to affect her strongly, however, and kept part of her thoughts turned always toward Grand Rapids.

In Vancouver, filming for *The X-Files*'s fourth season began in late July of 1996. Gillian's flirtation with stardom, represented by the *FHM* article, hung in the air. She still described herself as an outsider who had limited tolerance for the pretense and flippancy in the entertainment business. Nonetheless, she unveiled herself once again, in pictures and in copy, for the French publication, *MAX*.

French readers everywhere immediately compared her with famous European model Pamela Anderson, and not because the two coincidentally shared the same last name. Though Gillian's body was not as sculpted as Pamela's, her allure had an equally potent effect on men.

"I feel comfortable with the way that I look, the way that I dress, the way that I am," Gillian told *MAX*. "At twenty-

seven, I've had time to get used to my looks. I've been told that I'm an 'unconventional beauty,' and that doesn't displease me."

At first she had taken that particular comment as an insult, because it seemed a queer way to compliment somebody. She knew she wasn't the kind of woman that network executives were drawn to, but she felt appealing in her own way.

But by then, there were men out there who found her more than merely appealing. They daydreamed about her and her character, Dana Scully.

"I don't quite understand how the viewers see Dana Scully that way," she told *MAX*. Was it possible that someone could be very sexy without ideal beauty? "I think that there's a kind of aura about Scully." An aura Gillian found baffling.

What was harder to believe was that people could daydream about Gillian Anderson. She had felt cautious about the British calling her the Thinking Man's Crumpet, yet she preferred that to being labeled a bombshell, as Pamela

Anderson was. "I wouldn't want to be known as a body," she told *MAX*. "I want to be known for more than the size of my breasts."

> **She still described herself as an outsider who had limited tolerance for the pretense and flippancy in the entertainment business.**

A MORE MAINSTREAM AUDIENCE

Gillian celebrated her twenty-eighth birthday in early August. For a present, someone gave her the option of having a body piercing of her choice. She was thinking about it. "I have this little flap of skin at the top of my bellybutton, which I guess some people do and some people don't, but it just seems such a perfect place to pierce. But I've never seen anyone with an 'out-y' bellybutton pierced," she told *FHM*. She would later pose for *US* magazine in nothing but bikini panties and a mesh top, the hem pulled up to show her new bellybutton ring.

But for the time being, all such concerns had to be put aside as the season premiere aired in September. By then, *The X-Files* was a worldwide triumph. Shown in sixty countries, the drama was seen by sixteen million people every week. That fall of 1996, it moved from its Friday night slot on the Fox channel to Sunday nights, making way for Chris Carter's new *Millennium* series. Also, making it possible to gain a more mainstream audience. Friday night's cult show turned into a mainstream hit.

Scully and Mulder went on investigating cases that were fraught with danger both from the murky events they investigated and their truth-suppressing associates in the FBI. After three seasons, fans were aware of Agent Dana Scully's conversational tics, like the way she often restated the storyline about seventeen minutes into the show. And the way she clarified problems. Were Mulder to say, "We have a dead battery," she would say, "Mulder, what you're saying is that our battery has no electrical charge capable of furnishing a current."

Gillian claimed that Scully had laughed only once in three previous years—seventy-three installments— and smiled maybe three times. Chris Carter disagreed. Surely she had smiled more than that. Why, she'd even smiled in the pilot.

Very few *X-Files* characters smiled, though. The show was serious. And Scully's nature was to be serious anyway. She was a forensic pathologist, trying to deal with a partner who had eccentric, if not lunatic, ideas.

Gillian was no longer worried about typecasting, at least. Certainly, that had happened to the characters in the *Star Trek* series. They were extremely famous, yet couldn't get other parts. As David Duchovny had explained in so teacherly a manner at the Museum of Television

and Radio affair, *The X-Files,* unlike *Star Trek,* was really allegorical; the people and events were symbolic of ideas and principles. "[Gillian and I] are not playing . . . archetypical figures or action heroes . . . we're trying to portray regular human beings in dramatic and extreme situations. So, in that sense, I would hope we wouldn't be typecast." Also, according to Robert Goodman, co-executive producer, Scully and Mulder displayed a great depth; they weren't two-dimensional.

Gillian was being sent scripts. What was offered was a far cry from the quality of *The X-Files,* however. Besides, she didn't have the time to do the kind of auditioning that other actresses did.

The X-Files continued to receive awards and nominations. What more could Gillian want?

Sleep! She sometimes felt that her *X-Files* character was consuming her. She felt suffocated. It was stress, primarily. The hours and the arduous work and so much press. Constantly having someone say, Gillian, give an interview . . . answer these questions, was exhausting.

Tired as she might be, Gillian was still doing a lot of publicity. The redheaded actress had recently been posed in a "New York street" wearing little more than a pair of black gloves and some transparent slacks. As outlandish as the scene was, Gillian's concern was more about the brisk breeze than the fact that she was surrounded by strangers.

But nothing was as it seemed.

The New York street was a set designer's construction found in Twentieth Century Fox Studios in Century City (Los Angeles). *NYPD Blue* was shot there, and sometimes *Chicago Hope*. The likeness to a big city street was remarkable, however, even down to the graffiti on the buildings (cautiously rendered to ensure against inflaming gang passions). Gillian was there to be photographed for the British magazine, *Esquire*.

She had by then acquired the obligatory squad of publicists, stylists, and makeup artists, plus their assistants and their assistants' assistants.

"You're a breast man!" she accused the photographer when he rejected a cleavage-unfriendly dress. "You're enough to drive a woman to implants."

Everyone laughed at her jokes, as they might for a movie star. Of course, Gillian wasn't a movie star; she was a TV celebrity, yet possibly the world's most acclaimed female TV celebrity of the moment.

SPOKEN LINES

Gillian did agree to host a nine-part BBC documentary series about the curious and the unexplained: "If you've ever wondered whether the science of tomorrow can fulfill the spectacular promises of today's science fiction, then welcome to *The Future Fantastic*."

Five of the series' nine parts were shown on The Learning Channel in March 1997. The programs explored the close relationship between science fiction and science fact. It compared the ideas of visionaries to the work being done inside high-tech labs, work that pressed the limits of scientific inquiry.

Episode one, "Aliens," asked such questions as, What if extraterrestrials are hiding clues for us out in the universe's

> **" Gillian wasn't familiar with a computer-geek's ability to manipulate images. "**

though time travel remains beyond our technology, that may not always be so. Meanwhile, space is out there for the taking. Conquering the moon is the obvious first milestone. Where the pioneers advance, settlers will follow, and what was once the privilege of astronauts is our fantastic future.

unimaginable vastness, messages safely camouflaged until we are advanced enough to find them? Gillian pointed out that some evidence has been present all along. "It's just been covered up. Someone is not being straight with us."

Episode two was titled "The Incredible Shrinking Planet," and the third was "I, Robot," which pointed out that we are entering an exciting field of science where old rules are dissolving. In robotics, anything seems possible. So far robots have been glued to the factory assembly line, all muscle and no mind; but limb by limb, scientists are piecing together a more humanoid robot.

In the fourth episode, "Space Pioneers," space travel was discussed. Gillian quipped, "We're gonna need something faster, Scotty." She pointed out that

The fifth episode was "Immortals," and another program, shown in Great Britain but not the United States, was called "Why Planes Go Down." In the latter, Gillian said, "Over and over we hear that flying is the safest way to travel, based on the number of people who fly each year in the United States. Your chances are three million to one that a major carrier or commuter crash will kill you. Those are pretty great odds, but tell that to the hundreds of passengers who went down on these devastated flights."

Gillian also came out with a recorded single, related to the *Future Fantastic* broadcasts. She thought the series' sound track was fabulous and kept asking about the music. Finally, she suggested to the producer that he put together a CD, and he asked if she would be willing to do some vocals on it. He presented her with samples of spoken lines that she found poetic and erotic. An ambient group called Hal did the music, and the result was an outstanding dance single released in March 1997. A music video followed. When Gillian saw the original version of that, she called for modifications. "It's all me," she told *US*. "All me in every respect, and it's a bit too erotic for what I need to be doing right now. It's going to change."

This wasn't a new career, by any means. The politics of doing much else besides *The X-Files* were difficult. Switching between networks was frowned upon, "which is a real shame, because I'd love to do an episode of *Seinfeld*," she told *FHM*.

WHEN DID I SIT WITH MY KNEES OPEN?

She kept feeling aftershocks of that eye-popping, clothes-shedding cover story in *FHM*. Even months later, people occasionally approached her with copies they wanted signed.

But not all the jolts were that mundane. The magazine's photos had spawned many a sexual fantasy, which in turn spawned some salacious pranks. She came across a picture scanned from *FHM* on the Internet. Some socially stunted male had doctored it, in digital lechery, to look as if she'd pulled her bra down to expose her breasts—blown up as if with implants, not her own modest but natural ones. It was presented as if genuine. Her manager saw it and called to ask if she'd actually posed for such a photo.

There was another photo of her on the *X-Files* set, sitting with her legs open, her panties displayed. Her first thought was, Oh God, how did somebody take this picture without my knowing?

Then she thought, Hang on, I don't ever sit like that. Besides, she wears nylons on-set. But she kept thinking, When did I sit with my knees open?

Gillian wasn't familiar with a computer-geek's ability to manipulate images. Technology had produced a new genre of pornography.

The photos that accompanied the magazine's article weren't the only problem. "Almost everything I said in that *FHM* article has been taken so out of context in every area in the world," she told the British publication's Anthony Noguera over the phone one evening. Filming on *The X-Files* had wrapped for the day, and she was at home. "I can't believe how many articles have taken the piece and blown it out of proportion."

Though *FHM* readers controversially voted her "The Sexiest Woman in the World" in 1996, she thought that weird. "That's so funny. I'm sitting here on my bed in jeans and a T-shirt, my daughter is playing downstairs, and I've been working a very long day. And it sounds like such a strange thing for someone to say right now."

She was neither leggy enough nor busty enough to be a sex symbol. Yet she

was referred to by computer fans—the Gillian Anderson Testosterone Brigade—as "IDDG," which meant Intellectually Drop-Dead Gorgeous.

Her irresolution about her fame continued. She wanted it, but she didn't. She definitely was tiring of the same old geriatric inquiries from journalists: Do you believe in UFOs? Will Mulder and Scully get together? She'd heard her responses to these and other standard questions so many times that she just couldn't give them anymore. She refused to review her childhood any further. After all, it was only about growing up. Those rowdy days were just boring now.

"The biggest misconception about me that's grown up out of the *FHM* piece is that I lost my virginity to a neo-Nazi," she went on to Anthony Noguera. "The truth is, I lost my virginity to a guy who later *became* a neo-Nazi. Which is not the same thing." Why, if she hated anyone, it was neo-Nazis, racists, any kind of white supremacist group. (And child molesters. She absolutely despised them.)

Other stories bothered her even more. In an airport en route to Tahiti, she found a New Zealand magazine that claimed she was battling the serious disease of anorexia. She supposedly had an express diet she was to follow and a trainer who visited her house every weekday. It quoted her as saying she once went on eating binges.

She couldn't believe the popular press could get away with outright lying about things she'd never said. "Believe me, I very nearly sued them," she told *FHM*.

SKIN ART

In Tahiti, Gillian found herself surrounded by a musical speech dialect that was almost unintelligible to her. It circulated at a machine-gun speed, and was somewhat bewildering. At night, the stars looked like dewdrops in the sky. In such an exotic atmosphere, and because she needed to let off steam, she did something reminiscent of her nose-piercing punk days: She got a tattoo. In a very innocent place, her inner right ankle.

She hesitated, because tattoos were so common just then—that was why she had eliminated her nose ring. But Tahiti claimed to be a birthplace of tattooing, and Gillian was suddenly infected with the desire to do something immoderate.

She chose a tribal design that was about an inch across and twice that long. An amazing Polynesian fellow named George, who was tattooed over half his body, did the artwork. He had fabricated his own equipment, which looked like a sewing needle connected to an old electric shaver with a ballpoint pen sheath that had a shish kebab poked through it. He powered this questionable assortment of odds and ends with a battery pack.

One could presume that George did not have a license from the health authorities to do skin art.

At least he was very fast. It took him about ten minutes. Even so, Gillian found the procedure painful. She had been smiling, but the pain sobered her instantly. It felt as if she were at the dentist, having a tooth drilled. She told *FHM* that throughout the process she thought, "Why the f— am I doing this?"

But when the tattoo was done, she wanted another one almost immediately. She found it addictive but decided to wait. If she did get one more in the future, she thought she would have it done in the small of her back, or below her bellybutton.

Chapter Nine

Cliff-Hanger

THE TAHITIAN TATTOO DID NOT CAUSE GILLIAN any difficulty at work. She could use a skin tape if the cameras needed an ankle shot. But other difficulties would soon pop up on the *X-Files* set.

David had contributed story ideas to the series' writers. But Gillian took credit for inadvertently creating the show's mythology episodes, as her pregnancy had required a contrivance malevolent enough to keep Scully offscreen for two weeks.

"There are certain people on the show who are aware of that, and there are certain people on the show who don't want to admit that," she told *Rolling Stone.*

Gillian and David remained friendly, though it was difficult to work with anyone that intensely every single day. Their relationship constantly changed, and on weekends and holidays they definitely did not hang out together—not after rubbing elbows all week.

The discrepancy between their wages began to rankle. Whereas she had once felt David's larger experience warranted his larger take, they were now in the fourth season of a two-person smash-hit series—and Gillian was slaving just as hard as David. She tried to handle it by privately making a statement to the network powers that the inequality was no longer acceptable.

David knew about this, but had yet to say anything to Gillian about it. That rankled, too. So, despite affection, there was also some friction.

David was obviously the favored child. Did he think he deserved to be? Did he feel he deserved more money because he was a man? Was he simply taking the easiest path—and the larger salary—and leaving her to fight her own battle for equality? Thoughts like these could hardly have sat well with Gillian.

She sincerely loved the people she worked with, however. "I don't have much experience with other crews, but regardless, this is the best possible crew that anyone could dream of working with," said Gillian to *The X-Files Official Magazine.* "So many of the guest stars who come up here comment on . . . the fact that it feels so much like a family. They *are* my family, and I love every single one of them, from the production assistants to the painters to all the office people."

During a promotional trip to Australia in October, a crowd of thousands in Brisbane mobbed Gillian. "It was very strange," she told *FHM*, "because I was originally told we were going to do an in-store appearance, and my experience with in-stores in the past had been from one in a small bookshop in Munich."

When she and her escorts arrived at the place, however, she realized it was a mall. She objected; whether upon advice from her publicist or from personal preference, she didn't make mall appearances. But the organizers said she couldn't back out because they were anticipating several thousand customers. Apparently, they didn't get many visiting celebrities down under, so those that did visit got the public excited. Gillian didn't want to disappoint anyone.

In the end, a mob of twelve thousand showed up. Twelve thousand fans, some of whom had driven long distances for the event, all apparently looking for the Holy Grail of Gillian Anderson.

It quickly got messy. As Gillian appeared, the casual group suddenly galvanized. An instant of petrifying attention, all heads swiveling toward her, and then . . . everyone running. The screaming fans surged toward the stage, crushing teenagers at the front. Gillian tried to control them, saying that she'd love to stay and sign autographs, but that people were being hurt. In the end, the best thing she could do was leave.

Some of the fans had to be hospitalized, though police later reported there were no serious injuries.

THE SITUATION SUCKED

In Gillian's mind, the mobbing in Australia was not due to her personal appearance. She felt the response would have been the same for any representative of *The X-Files*. She did *not* want to believe twelve thousand people would behave like that just for her. That would make her somebody she didn't want to be. She had seen the huge temptation in her business for people to let such things inflate their heads. She tried to keep her fame in perspective. Gillian wanted to remain humble, to simply appreciate what had come her way.

She couldn't believe she was such a big star. How could she be, when she herself was still starstruck by such actors

as Meryl Streep, Jessica Lange, Gary Oldman, and Robert De Niro?

"I'm impressed by people who make a difference. People who are really good at what they do. People like Tim Robbins, Jodie Foster, Quentin Tarantino," she told *FHM*.

She also admired Isabelle Adjani, whose performance in *Camile Claudel* had a huge impact on her. Gillian loved Emma Thompson and thought Patricia Arquette was amazing in *True Romance*.

She practically worshipped Gary Oldman. He could do no wrong, especially since he'd quit drinking. She knew many actors feared that if they gave up an addictive crutch, they'd lose some vital edge. Gillian didn't believe that. She felt it took more guts to remain awake and fully conscious in that business.

Back on the set after her October visit to Australia, there were cracks forming in the *X-Files* dike. Chris Carter had been dividing his time between the show's fourth season and his new project, *Millennium*. In fact, Chris's professional life

> **"** She was tired of Mulder always saving Scully's bacon and would like Scully to do the lifesaving more often. **"**

was developing almost like an *X-Files* plot: a massive international business feeding out of one man's anxieties.

David Duchovny told *Rolling Stone*, "[Chris has] been with us less than during the first three seasons. And I think that if the quality of the show hasn't suffered, definitely the process of making the episodes has become harder, just because Chris is very controlling and wants to be. But he doesn't have the time now."

Gillian had some complaints about the structure of the show as well. She was tired of Mulder always saving Scully's bacon and would like Scully to do the lifesaving more often. When a fan called a CBC talk show to complain about the same situation, Gillian answered, "I don't know if it's necessarily her needing to be

rescued, or the writers needing to see her being rescued by a man."

Gillian wanted Scully to "kick ass" periodically. The only episode in which she'd done that recently was when a man tried to suck the fat out of Scully's body—his regular means of survival. Then Scully got to do some major ass-kicking.

Gillian also complained to *Rolling Stone* about an element that was in far too many installments over the four years: "At one point, Mulder will speak, and Scully says, 'And where are you going? What are you doing? You're going to do what?' He's leading, and I'm back here being told what to do. You know, that sentence is in almost every single episode." She actually put together a collection of those clips to run when she did Jay Leno's show. They ran a blooper tape instead.

Gillian was also finding it harder to continue as the skeptic. She had several conversations with Chris, in which she expressed concern that the audience was laughing at Scully because she repeated herself over and over.

But Gillian's main grievance continued to be the salary variance. Although she'd taken pains to keep her protests private, somehow the situation got public.

So be it. Gillian couldn't back down. She was fighting more for equality than money. She was, she freely admitted, adequately compensated for her work, yet she resented the crafty and duplicitous machinations of television contracts, which treated women like second-class performers. In other words, the situation sucked.

Gillian was living proof that gender inequities lived on in Hollywood despite the women's liberation movement. It was apparent that women had to look a certain way to get good roles—Gillian knew of only one successful larger-than-average female actress, Kathy Bates. And whereas male performers could look any way they wanted and continue to work regularly into old age, for women over a certain age, there were only one or two good parts a year.

Then there were the limited roles available to actresses. Women were constantly characterized as sidekicks, ingenues, and mere accessories to males, rarely as independent, capable individuals.

And to bring it full circle, the discrepancies in pay were tremendous. The amounts some male performers made were obscene. Even stars such as Julia Roberts and Goldie Hawn weren't earning what their masculine counterparts were.

Gillian's dissatisfaction went deep. She told *US*, "I wanted out more than anything. I didn't talk about it with many people, but I was *so* ready to walk."

WITHOUT CLYDE

A lot of people came up to her and quietly said they were glad she was taking a stand. Yet it obviously wasn't doing any good. Rumors abounded: Gillian might leave; Fox might write her out of the series.

It was ironic. While Dana Scully broke television stereotypes, Gillian battered her head against a glass ceiling. It was scary, scarier than any episode of *The X-Files*.

At home, Gillian found more problems. She and Clyde separated in October. Although Gillian gave no explanation for the breakup, she had recently admitted to *TV Guide* that she was hard to be married to.

"Anybody in the situation I'm in right now would be hard to be married to. I'm incredibly strong-willed. I want to do what I want to do. I'm not controlling, but I know what I want."

In November, Gillian revealed publicly her complaint that David was still being paid about double what she was. If the Fox network didn't raise her earnings closer to David's, well, something would have to be done.

Though her current contract was far from over, she was determined to find salary parity. Would she succeed? Some said that the network threatened to write Scully out of the show, but the program's continuing success and Gillian's role in that spoke loudly that she might soon be in a higher tax bracket.

"At this point, you can't imagine anybody else playing [Scully's] part. There's not just one thing she does. She's made it her own part. So, there's nobody else to do it," David said of Gillian to *US*.

The filming year of *The X-Files* was punishing, and by the last location filming before Christmas, the employees of Ten-Thirteen Productions were restless. That episode's script had Gillian and David lifting an extremely realistic head out of a stainless steel tub. The two actors were having a hard time, and the special-effects man was concerned about the head.

After four years, the leads had worked out some complicated patterns in their relationship. At times they could be very aligned, and at others they were in completely different worlds, just showing up to do their jobs. When Chris Mundy, writing for *US*, got the stars together for a rare dual interview, he said they sat down like polite family members who had come together out of respect for their mutual obligations. At other times there could be an oddly crafty feel to their interaction.

"It's a difficult relationship because it's like an arranged marriage," David said. "We didn't choose to be together."

Fans wanted them to be great friends. Or be fighting. But the two simply didn't socialize. They did have discussions, often about mending things the press had misquoted one saying about the other.

Finally, as the head rose out of the tub again, the stars struck their lines. It was a wrap. The special effects man sighed with relief, and within minutes, the staff was exchanging holiday farewells. The studio started emptying fast.

In her trailer, Gillian changed into street clothes to go home—a fuzzy sweater, jeans, her glasses, a baseball cap. She was no glamour-puss. Part of her charm was that she looked less like a star than a study partner.

"It's fun to dress up to a certain degree," she told *TV Guide*. "I wouldn't want to do it all the time."

Without Clyde, her plans for the Christmas break included two days at a Hindu ashram "I think that we are all connected by a universal rhythmic energy," she revealed to *Rolling Stone*.

Gillian had put off acting on many of her spiritual urges since *The X-Files* had usurped most of her life. The long hours of the show prohibited her from doing many activities, including charitable work—beyond sending an autographed photograph to a fund-raising auction when asked. Gillian would like to do much more. She favored causes that helped battered women; people with AIDS; and, of course, sufferers of neurofibromatosis, that rare disease that plagued her beloved brother.

NO NOSE RING

On January 13, 1997, the parting with Clyde became permanent. The news was made public in a British tabloid, and was confirmed by Gillian's publicist the next day. According to the publicist, the agreement to separate was an amiable one. Gillian would keep their two-year-old daughter.

On January 15, *The Los Angeles Times* listed the most recent week's prime-time TV rankings. After the usual Sunday football orgy, viewers had scattered to other shows. *Seinfeld*, the number one program, had been watched by nearly 34.5 million people. But *The X-Files* rose to its best-ever results. As number two program, 1,008,258 households had tuned in.

Gillian had no husband at her side for the 1996 Golden Globe ceremonies on January 20. She wore a simple low-cut gown—in black again, the favorite color of her punk-famed youth. Her only jewelry was a pair of glittering earrings. No nose ring in sight.

Evita and *The English Patient* won the top movie awards. In the eleven television categories, *The X-Files* swept the drama voting, taking awards for outstanding series and for best actress and actor.

In his acceptance speech, reported in *The Los Angeles Times*, David noted that

before *The X-Files* had premiered, he'd attended the Golden Globes once as someone's guest. "I never dreamed that I'd be up here six or seven years later holding one of these things."

In Clyde's absence, Gillian awarded her costar a lingering kiss, tempting fans to believe there was something finally gelling between the pair. It was only for the cameras, however. Gillian, now twenty-eight, and David, thirty-five, weren't lovers.

In the glow of the after-awards hours, Gillian and David both expressed reservations about continuing with *The X-Files* if creator and executive producer Chris Carter left, as he had recently stated he intended to do after the next (fifth) season.

In fact, as February came, rumors circulated more furiously that Gillian was exiting the show. Reasons included her wage dispute and her marital problems. Fans on the Internet circulated petitions in a frenzy to keep Gillian on the air.

Gossip disagreed on whether she was going anywhere. America Online as-

> **". . . Gillian awarded her costar a lingering kiss, tempting fans to believe there was something finally gelling between the pair."**

sured its "X-Files Forum" fans that Gillian wasn't being fired, wasn't quitting, and above all, her character was not being conveniently killed off. Her contract ran through a fifth season.

Another notice would soon appear in *Dish Entertainment* magazine, however, warning fans of *The X-Files* to beware. "The hit Fox show may be yanked from its Sunday night time slot and off the air altogether. Why? Well, they want the show to go off a huge hit."

Gillian seemed to be proceeding as if she expected to film a fifth year of the series in the fall. In February, *Variety* reported that she had signed for her first film role. In *The Mighty* she would costar with Sharon Stone, Gena Rowlands, and Harry Dean Stanton. The Miramax Films movie concerned the journey of a boy whose physical growth stops at the age of six. Peter Chelsom would direct the screen version of Rodman Philbrick's novel. Gillian began work on it in late

March, anticipating the Fox drama's hiatus, beginning in April.

She took a role, as well, in an independent film, *Hellcab*, alongside John Cusack and Julianne Moore.

Gillian had room for one more movie on her TV break—if a mere break it was. Sources said she and costar David Duchovny would be busy on Chris Carter's *The X-Files* movie, which would begin filming immediately after the season wrapped production. Chris was traveling to Maui to write the screenplay from a story conceived with writer-producer Frank Spotnitz. The film would be guided by series director-producer Rob Bowman. Emmy-winner John Bartley might be director of cinematography.

However, the majority of the series' production team would not be involved, since they would be working on the TV show while the movie's prep work went forward during the hiatus. Gillian and David Duchovny would return for the show's fifth season in the fall, and Gillian would again take up the perils of Agent Scully.

Chris expected the film, tentatively scheduled for a summer or fall 1998 release, to serve as a resolution of the fifth-year cliff-hanger. Or would it have to be the fourth-year cliff-hanger?

ON THE BIG SCREEN

Gillian was sure *The X-Files Movie* would be successful. Why not? Everyone who had ever seen the show, and the quality of the work and production, would want to see it on the big screen. And Chris was sure to draft an amazing script, something dependably exciting, mysterious, scary, moody, intelligent, slick, chic, and complex. The Fox network would promote it like hell. If it happened they weren't doing the weekly shows any-

more, the audience would not have a weekly *X-Files* "fix." That humongous audience, which relied on the series being aired every single week, would come to the theaters in droves.

Of course, because Fox owned *The X-Files*, even the concept, there was always the slight chance that once Gillian and David departed, the network could launch new stars, whether in feature films or the TV series. Fox could conceivably set up two new FBI agents to handle *The X-Files*, in the same way that *Star Trek* kept gaining new crews.

Gillian didn't think that that would be successful, not because she and David necessarily made the show, but because the audience wouldn't be able to make that transition. The fans really controlled the show, as much as they relied on it to be there and were disappointed if there were reruns. The truth was, many people were just plain addicted to it.

Gillian continued to learn interesting items about herself through reading the popular press. Her stardom made her a prime target for many tabloids. *Hard Copy* called her a sexpot. Rumors said she had left Clyde for Adrian Hughes, thirty-two, an *X-Files* bit player in the "Home" episode. However, according to the more sober *Parade* magazine, Adrian told Vancouver reporters, "Gillian Anderson and I are just friends." Whatever the relationship was, Gillian soon dumped her "friend," learning he was charged with sexual assault. His trial was set for April 14, 1997.

Her popularity brought about retail sales of an independent film made before her graduation from college in which she'd had a small role. In her first camera work, *The Turning*, she played a tiny part as an ingenue. There was a very innocent love scene between Gillian's character and her sweetheart. He took Gillian's shirt off, and viewers could see her naked back. Though British papers called it a porn film, Gillian feared that those who bought it for titillation would be sorely disappointed.

On the good side of this avalanche of events, Gillian's episode of *The Simpsons* finally aired.

There simply was no time for her to examine any of these incidents in depth. Her whole life continued to revolve around her work on *The X-Files*. Yet she never went home after her sixteen hours on the set to dream *The X-Files*–type dreams. "The only time I have nightmares is when I wake up knowing that I haven't prepared enough for the next day's shooting," she told *FHM*. Mostly, however, her dreams weren't disturbing. She was too tired.

Nonetheless, sometimes she had a hard time falling asleep at night and found that having the television on made her doze off easier. Otherwise, she didn't keep up with television. She'd never been a regular viewer, and probably would not have caught *The X-Files* shows if Scully's part had gone to someone else. The series was not something that would have attracted her at all.

By her fourth year on the show, she had become immune to the subject matter in *The X-Files*. "I honestly don't give a s— how people perceive it," was the way she put it to *FHM*. Although she knew people thought about it after watching it and found a lot in it, she honestly didn't care anymore. If they enjoyed it as entertaining hokum or serious food for thought, it made no difference to her.

Perhaps this lack of interest was why she could finally watch herself playing Scully. At first she couldn't. And she still couldn't watch early episodes. They were in the past, and she thought they were bad.

Chapter Ten

Other Roles

GILLIAN'S CAREER HAD REACHED SUCH A POINT of mass that it was snowballing without her conscious efforts. A new CD-ROM based on the flying war game, Hellbender, was released by Microsoft and Terminal Reality, and the aspect that many of its players liked most was the voice of the EVE (Enhanced Virtual Entity) computer. The voice was Gillian's. Reviewer Bob Woods wrote, "If my computer could sound like that all of the time, I'd more than just enjoy using it—I'd love it as much as humanly possible."

On March 15, 1997, Gillian—with Will Smith *(Independence Day)*, Steven Spielberg, and other celebrities—helped open the video mall of the future, GameWorks, in Seattle, Washington. Performers rapped and rocked for a live MTV telecast of the premier of the huge indoor multimedia amusement park, and Gillian was able to abandon her serious *X-Files* persona for a virtual water-scooter ride.

Gillian had no trouble having fun. Unlike Special Agent Scully, who might be the least humorous woman on television, with her serious suits and drab pumps and self-righteous discipline, the real-life Gillian was ready to join almost any amusement. The GameWorks opening was right up her fun-loving alley.

Dozens of GameWorks were planned across the country, offering as many as 250 advanced video games, a slew of theme restaurants, and a brew pub in The Loft. It was an update of the traditional arcade and meant to appeal to young adults who could drop up to five dollars per whack at virtual reality and the newest cutting-edge games.

This first one was located at 7th and Pike in Seattle and occupied a 30,000-square-foot industrial space.

While Gillian flew her virtual water scooter solo, Smith faced computer mogul Bill Gates in a race à la the Indy 500. Starbucks workers kept the notables in coffee from large buckets carried on their backs. "This is definitely the night-club of the future," Smith told a *Sacramento Bee* reporter.

During the event, the computer-shy Gillian communicated live with fans via America Online, an experience in virtual reality in itself. Fans online were "seated" in "rows." They could submit questions to hostesses, who then interfaced with Gillian. The event was so well attended that room in the arena was limited. One sly latecomer with no seat posed as an AOL official and sent a message to an already seated attendee that a technical problem required the attendee to move. The incident illustrated that things in cyberspace weren't all that different from the real world.

Soon Gillian made her appearance. What was she wearing? Perhaps a snug pink cardigan, unbuttoned enough to show a peek of black bra beneath? What was her demeanor? In person in the real world, she's said to drop Scully's schoolmarm frumpiness, though not her intensity.

Questions gathered by the hostesses were presented to her. The first: How was motherhood treating her?

"Fabulously," she answered.

She explained she was not a geek, the term used for lovers of technology. "I like it, but I don't participate." Though she had never said so explicitly, those who read between the lines of her various statements about the Internet could gather that she preferred to avoid that paranoid army of keyboard fans who punched shift keys and double-clicked mice in quest of increasing levels of Gillian Anderson and *X-Files* minutiae. What *could* she think of Web sites called "The Church of the Immaculate Gillian," "The Gillian Anderson Testosterone Brigade" (formed as a backlash to the "David Duchovny Estrogen Brigade"), and "The Gillian Anderson Estrogen Brigade" formed by women who prefer women?

Asked if there were any similarities between the character of Scully and herself, her humor peeked through. "We have the same hair color," she answered. Even in cyberspace, her laughter was heard.

BONES TO GNAW

She assured her cyberspace audience that she planned to continue the *X-Files* show at least one more year. Asked which episodes she found most challenging to film, she answered, "'Memento Mori'—and the kitty cat episode, too." Her favorite episodes were "Ice," "Piper Maru" (titled after her daughter), "Memento Mori," and "Jose Chung's *From Outer Space*."

What other roles would she like to be cast in? "Kate, in *The Taming of the Shrew*." She added, "Movies are in the works."

What three recordings would she bring to a desert island? Cake's "Fashion Nugget," Emmy Lou Harris's "Wrecking Ball," and Jane Siberry's "When I Was a Boy."

What ever happened to the tattoo Scully got in the episode, "Never Again"? "She still has it," Gillian replied.

She admitted she sometimes gets tired of doing *The X-Files.*

Asked what is the biggest fear in her life, she said, "Fear itself." And to the question if she'd learned anything from this character Scully she answered, "To be fearless!"

One fan wondered, "How do we know this is really Gillian Anderson?" (A better question might have been, how did *she* know she was Gillian Anderson? as the last few years had altered her life beyond recognition.) Gillian's humor flashed again, "You can tell by my mole, on my upper lip."

Why did she think she and David worked so well together? "I have no idea . . . but thank heavens!"

And, yes, she still kept in touch with everyone she used to before she became famous.

> **"** About the single question that fans most avidly ask—did Dana and Fox love each other—she said she thought they did. **"**

Then she was gone. The computers across America seemed somehow less alive. But the "geeks" had some bones to gnaw, and they would gnaw them for days to come.

On April 24, Gillian played a special role, in the fifth annual Take Our Daughters to Work Day. She was joined by actress Marlo Thomas, opera star Jessye Norman, Ann Reinking from the Broadway hit "Chicago," designer Kate Spade, and writer Gloria Steinem. Each of the six celebrities served as a mentor for a girl in Los Angeles or New York. The girls were selected by the *Ms.* magazine's Foundation for Women on the basis of their essays about how this annual event had affected their lives. Gillian volunteered because she considered it a positive experience for American girls. For one day in April she could give up the hunt for aliens to help with the development of a very human young girl.

The star's favorite charity remained Neurofibromatosis, Inc. In May, Neurofibromatosis Month, Cyndi Schmidt, webmistress for the "Gillian Anderson Web Site," collected donations to be sent to NF, Inc. in Gillian's name.

But what about *The X-Files*? Was it going to be archived like the alien fetus that Cancer Man filed away in a huge Pentagon basement during the end of "The Erlenmeyer Flask" episode?

Gillian had told *Rolling Stone* that she believed in the show, saying, "I think it is excellent." And she was devoted to Chris. Also, "I own a house in Vancouver. So I basically live here." She felt Vancouver would always be a nostalgic spot for her. She'd learned to appreciate even the cloudy weather that made the sun so scrumptious whenever it did glow momentarily.

"And you know, the closer we get to the end, the more I start to realize what an important part of my life this has been.

"But I do believe that we should not go on any longer than we . . . can hold up the quality of the work that we're doing." She was aware of the singularity of the *X-Files* phenomenon, "and it is better to leave with a bang than with a fizzle."

About the single question that fans most avidly ask—did Dana and Fox love each other—she said she thought they did. "They're not *in* love . . . but I think they have great love for each other."

Fans of the show thought they wanted them to fall "in" love. But would they be pleased with the after effects? Gillian believed not. "It is tantalizing to them when we are intimate in any way. But if we were actually to end up together, the excitement would last only for as long as the episode. And so it would be a disappointment."

Once asked by CBC's Virginia Campbell if Scully didn't work with Mulder would she fall for him, Gillian

had replied, "I don't think so. Mulder's hip. It's their work that makes them attracted to each other."

HAVING SEX WITH SCULLY

Chris Carter spoke of Scully and Mulder's connection on the show as an ideal version of a couple—without the sex, but very close and protective. Chris told *Rolling Stone*, "My feeling is that the most powerful relationships you have in your life are . . . not sexual."

Gillian tentatively agreed. "I think that would be a very good place to be. I've always wanted a relationship of two individuals coming together." After the experience of her failed marriage, she dreamed of a relationship in which each person did her or his own thing, coming together only for certain shared experiences that made them close—a relationship in which the partners were supportive of each other, not bolted at the hip or each other's keeper.

David Duchovny had said he would like to see the series end with Mulder having sex with Scully and then dying. Gillian agreed at least that Scully and Mulder could finally consummate their famously non-intimate relationship at the end. She would like to finish with them in bed losing nine minutes of time, bringing them full circle from the pilot episode. They wake up and don't quite know what's happened in those lost minutes.

Chris Carter maintained that he would resist that idea. Asked at an America Online conference when the two characters would get together, he had replied, "When hell freezes over." But he also said, enigmatically, that was what the *X-Files* movies would be for.

Meanwhile, Gillian's real-life relationship with David seemed to go on as always: fine.

That Dana and Fox were considered television's most romantic duo was a feat of pure dramatic genius, considering the two characters never so much as kissed. And considering the two totally different people who played them, it was stranger still. While Scully and Mulder were the greatest of friends, David and Gillian were the greatest of acquaintances.

As for fan mail, Gillian was getting more than ever. Whereas once it had been manageable, suddenly it wasn't manageable at all. She couldn't quite figure out a remedy. She couldn't conceive of hiring somebody to feign her signature. She would rather grab a few letters, when she had the chance, and write responses herself.

Gillian continued to take her daughter to the set every day. In general, Piper didn't mind the freaky, frightening stuff. Someone with blood oozing out of her ears or an eyeball down on his cheek could approach her, and though she might be cautious, all she would say was, "Owie."

A gross understatement.

As much an understatement as saying that success had changed Gillian. She was not as accepting as she once was. She needed her space and hated crowds at work. She was less tolerant of giving autographs during the breaks between takes. And less tolerant of people snapping pictures of her in the street.

Naturally, she couldn't tell anyone what she knew about the future of *The*

X-Files. She'd used her spiky humor to put off David Letterman's questions, saying, "Do you really expect me to tell you what happens on the show? I can't tell you, Dave. I can't tell you. If I tell you, I will have to kill you."

When CBC asked her what was going to happen, she said, blandly, that the characters would chase bogeymen, face death, and . . . live.

Indeed, they would, in at least one movie, and in video collections of the series. Gillian would be seen as Scully for a very long time.

Meanwhile, the principal players, Gillian, David, and Chris, were all following leads toward fresh career paths. "I don't want to be known as just a TV star," Gillian told *MAX.* And as her career became more established, she looked forward to dividing her time more equally among work, family, and volunteer activities. And to becoming more selective about roles. The script would be what was most important. She likes movies that have something to say—or that say nothing extremely well, like *Pulp Fiction.*

Ability to project gravity and humanity being so deficient among young screen performers, Hollywood would no doubt find roles that called for a younger, softer-edged Meryl Streep.

"Also, I'd like to eventually get back into doing theater in New York," she told *Rolling Stone.*

UNIVERSAL ENLIGHTENMENT AND A FAIR PAYCHECK

She'd never stayed put in one place for long. From Chicago to Puerto Rico, then London, Grand Rapids, Chicago, again New York, Los Angeles, and on to Vancouver—and she still got restless. Always restless for new accomplishments. Thirsty to play another character; to show people that she was *able* to play another character. And to prove it to herself.

Would she continue to be a sex symbol? Never having any idea what it was about her that provoked such male interest, she felt the whole thing was a mistake—or a gag. It was hugely flattering, but sometimes annoying, too, as

> **"** Twice she'd mistakenly believed nobody was around snapping pictures, and pictures showed up. **"**

when she couldn't take a vacation without being followed. Twice she'd mistakenly believed nobody was around snapping pictures, and pictures showed up. That was upsetting, really upsetting.

However, she told the British *Esquire*, "This is my life's work. This is what I know how to do, and what I care about as much as anything in my life. I'm not going to give it up because I can't handle the attention. It's about following one's heart and one's dream. It's not about fame."

Yet her photo materialized on the cover of *Esquire* topless but for strategically crossed arms. She'd posed for it. Not the act of someone who really believed it wasn't about fame—or, at least attention. More likely, it *was* about fame. And

she would miss it if it were to vanish from her life as suddenly as it had appeared.

It could disappear. The capricious tornado of celebrity might very well dump her after *The X-Files*'s demise, as suddenly as it had whirled her headlong into stardom.

If such a fear lurked in her mind, for the moment she had her work cut out for her in the projects she had pending. She didn't want much from life—only universal enlightenment and a fair paycheck. . . .

Meanwhile, whether *The X-Files* would film a fifth season's episodes or move into a feature film format for good, Gillian told *The X-Files Official Magazine*, "The closer we get to the end, even if it's another year, or two years, the more I stop to think—[despite the occasional] hassle and the weather and the hours, I realize that these are going to be the best years of our lives."

Scully in Review

SEASON ONE
The X-Files Pilot

The pilot is what hooked many future X-Philes and made them want to watch one episode after another. Scully is relaxed in this first episode, not too professional. Her behavior matches Mulder's cynicism well.

FBI Special Agent Dana Scully (M.D.) is assigned a partner—infamous fellow-agent Fox "Spooky" Mulder, who is working on cases classified as "X-files" because they seem unsolvable. Scully's job is to watch, evaluate, and report on her new partner.

She finds Mulder wary of her. They travel to Oregon to investigate a series of deaths that Mulder believes may involve alien abduction. Scully argues for a more rational explanation.

All the victims have sported marks on their backs, which Mulder attributes to alien experimentation. The sexual tension that becomes famous between the two agents makes its first notable appearance on Mulder's face when Scully strips to the waist for him to examine a mark she's found on the small of her back. Obviously she's letting his beliefs influence her already.

Scully reports to her superiors that although she believes Mulder's theories, she can't prove them. But after this episode, her willingness to believe disappears again.

Worst line: Scully's, "Are you able to breathe?"

Best line: "I even made my parents call me Mulder."

<SCULLYISM>

Sardine juice, half a dozen lemons, and the water from a snow globe.

Plot problem: Scully and Mulder pull a girl out of a river and start life-saving procedures. They give up too soon. Scully is a doctor and should know that CPR can revive a victim as long as forty-five minutes after normal breathing stops.

To look for: Scully's quote from *Close Encounters of the Third Kind.*

Deep Throat

Like too many of the first season episodes, this one is underrated.

Scully and Mulder travel to a U.S. Air Force base in Idaho to investigate the strange disappearances of test pilots. They witness what appear to be UFOs flying openly above the base. Men in Black (see "X-Talk") appear to discourage their inquiries. One of them removes the magazine from Scully's gun, leaving her helpless to stop them from beating Mulder.

Though Scully warns Mulder to leave while he still has a job, he infiltrates a secret area where he finds a UFO. Scully ignores protocol to get him back.

Best line: "You've seen things that weren't meant to be seen."

Squeeze

The opening sequence of this episode is one of the eeriest and most memorable ever seen on any TV series.

Scully is approached by an old FBI pal. He tips her off to an unusual case involving victims whose livers have been removed, evidently by someone with the strength to tear into their bodies bare-handed. Scully and Mulder can find only one elongated fingerprint at the crime scene.

The fingerprint matches those found at similar murders occurring every thirty years.

They soon capture Eugene Tooms attempting to crawl down an air vent. But they must release him. Afterward, however, they find that when stretched by computer graphics his fingerprint matches the elongated one.

The agents visit a man who investigated a past set of these bizarre murders. His help leads them to a slimy nest in a condemned building where Mulder is forced to ask Scully how he can look cool with bile all over his fingers.

Attempting to make Scully his victim, Tooms attacks her in her apartment. Mulder calls to warn her, but Tooms has cut Scully's phone line. (Why doesn't he try her cellular phone?) Eventually he does arrive in time to help her apprehend Tooms.

An intriguing episode.

Conduit

A girl disappears on a camping trip. Scully wants to write it off as a kidnapping and murder. Mulder sees chilling signs of alien involvement.

Scully detects the most important clue: The missing girl's brother, serving as a conduit, provides a picture of his sister derived from a binary code he "hears" through a static-filled TV screen.

This episode introduces Mulder's primary motivation as an investigator—his belief that his sister was abducted while he watched helplessly. His hypnotic-regression tapes about Samantha Mulder's abduction are played. Mulder cries while Scully listens.

The Jersey Devil

Scully and Mulder travel to New Jersey to investigate the death of a man in a state park. The partially eaten body suggests human cannibalism. Dismissing Mulder's hypothesis about a Jersey Devil as mere legend, Scully goes to her godson Trent's birthday party.

While Scully works on her social life, Mulder works on the case without her. Luckily, she returns in time to frighten off a beast-woman attacking him.

Shadows

A forgettable week on *The X-Files*. The team is called to Philadelphia to examine the bodies of two thieves killed by an apparently mysterious force. Scully examines the very odd corpses.

A surveillance videotape leads her and Mulder to a secretary. This woman is then visited by the ghost of her dead boss, who tells her he was murdered by his partner. She confronts the partner and is consequently attacked because of her suspicions. But the attackers meet the same fate as the earlier thieves.

To look for: The boss died on the fifth of the month. Scully's journal in the next episode, "Ghost in the Machine," is dated the fourth of the same month. And the security video showing the secretary being attacked is dated 09/22/93, though it is supposedly two weeks after the boss's death.

Ghost in the Machine

This episode is not the best, but there are some interesting moments.

A computer company's CEO has been electrocuted, and Mulder's old partner, Jerry Lamana, asks for help with the case. With the advice of Deep Throat, Scully and Mulder must stop the murderer, all the while fighting off the defense department—and the actual building itself, which is run by a high-tech, artificial-intelligence computer that Mulder believes is sentient. (Chris Carter's version of HAL in Kubrick and Clark's *2001*?)

Mulder tries to do a little investigating on his own, and when Scully drives up, his frustrated sigh is funny and revealing; she's slowly pushing her way into his life.

In another scene, as Scully and Mulder buy lunch, an old boss, Reggie Purdue, interrupts. When he hugs Mulder, the looks Scully and Mulder exchange are amusing and foreshadow their deepening relationship.

Of course, Scully doesn't believe Mulder's theory about the computer. But the two are bonding as partners. When Lamana dies, Scully comforts Mulder.

Scully seems more human in this episode than in others.

Best scene: As Scully and Mulder drive into the dangerous building and something flies down at them.

Plot problems: First, although the scene in which Scully gets into the HVAC ductwork and battles the fan is a good one, that kind of system could not possibly generate enough airspeed or flow to move a person.

Second, why do Scully and Mulder have to go through a security gate to get to the building when Lamana is able to follow the building's designer right to the doors?

Third, how does the Eurisko computer turn on Scully's machine? Although there are devices that can remotely turn on computers, Scully wouldn't have one of those on her system. Also, when the Eurisko calls her computer, the phone rings on her bedside cabinet, which shows she has only one line into her home. When she goes to her computer and sees her files being accessed, why doesn't she just unplug the computer's modem from the phone socket? Instead, she picks up the phone to call for a trace, but the phone line should still be busy with modem squeaks.

Ice

One of the best episodes ever.

A haggard man makes a videotape of himself, saying, "We are not who we are." While taping, he's interrupted by another man. They fight—then back away from each other and, in silent agreement, commit suicide.

A pilot called Bear flies Scully, Mulder, and three other scientists to Icy Cape, Alaska, to investigate the deaths.

Scully's examination of the corpses reveals a small single-celled organism and the presence of ammonia in the blood.

Meanwhile, Bear grows violent and attacks Mulder. As Bear is restrained, Scully notices movement under the skin at the base of his neck. She extracts a worm. Bear dies.

This parasite was unearthed—or un-iced—from deep in the arctic core. (Chris Carter's version of John Carpenter's *The Thing*.)

Scully works hard to discover a cure for infestation, which involves the insertion of a second worm into a victim's ear. (Chris's version of a certain *Star Trek* movie?)

Mulder's contact with Bear may have infected him. That

< S C U L L Y I S M >
That man is clearly delusional.

suspicion increases when Scully and the others find him with the dead body of one of their team. Scully and Mulder quarrel. She doesn't know if she can trust him. In order to protect herself and the others from harm, she pulls a gun on him. (Would she really shoot him? See the episode "Anasazi" to find out.)

The others gang up on Mulder and almost insert a parasite into his ear, but Scully stops them. She reasons they must give him one last chance. She'll lock him up and see if he shows signs of infestation. Risking herself, she enters the room in which they've locked him. She makes him turn around so she can check his nape. Seeing nothing, she's prepared to release him. But he wants to check her, as well; and these intimate touches—and the look on Scully's face—are classic restrained-erotic cinematics.

When the woman who is infested goes crazy, Mulder lunges across the room to tackle her.

In the end, Scully and Mulder are informed that the base has been torched by a U.S. government agency.

To look for: When the recording of the first scientist is played back to Scully, there's a pause that wasn't there before. Also, though it's summer in Nome, it seems to be winter in Icy Cape.

This episode shows that Gillian and David have the acting ability to pull off as many seasons of *The X-Files* as they want.

Space

After a United States space shuttle launch is aborted, a NASA worker asks the agents to investigate the possibility of some bizarre sabotage. Meanwhile, the astronaut formerly in charge of the mission is haunted by something encountered during a spacewalk. Examining the records, the agents realize the haunted astronaut is the saboteur.

Plot problem: Scully isn't always as commanding as a doctor normally would be. She tells paramedics to give the astronaut ten milligrams of a drug, and warns Mulder of an aneurysm, but later fails to give an astronaut simple first aid.

Fallen Angel

Deep Throat tips off Mulder about a government cover-up of a UFO crash site. The military keep him away while they try to capture a mysterious being at the site. Mulder is the one they catch, however.

Scully bails him out, informing him that he's in big trouble with FBI higher-ups.

A nice moment occurs as Mulder rushes Scully out of his motel room; she asks him if he's got a woman coming over.

Best speech: When Mulder says to his superiors, "You can deny all the things I've seen, all the things I've discovered . . . but not for much longer. Because too many other people know what's happening out there—and no one, no government agency, has jurisdiction over the truth."

Plot problem: The story of another UFO enthusiast, Max Fenig, is woven in, and when Scully finds a bottle of Melleril in his RV, she immediately concludes that he's schizophrenic. But that particular drug is used for other conditions as well.

To look for: When Scully and Mulder enter the motel room to find Max trying to wriggle out the window, Mulder goes for his gun, doesn't have it, and motions to Scully to draw hers. Later, Mulder has a gun again. Also, Mulder tells Scully that Max has an abduction scar behind his left ear, but when Max is lying on his bed, the scar is clearly behind his right ear.

A clever story, and great cinematography. The scene in which Scully faces the committee over a reflective table is exceptionally well done.

Eve

Scully and Mulder investigate the simultaneous and identical deaths of two men on opposite coasts. When one of the dead men's eight-year-old daughter is kidnapped a few days later, the agents travel from Connecticut to California to protect the other victim's eight-year-old. They discover the two girls are identical twins. Both families were involved in the same fertility program headed by Dr. Sally Kendrick, who was fired for unauthorized genetics experiments.

The partners find an identical twin of Kendrick in Litchfield, an asylum for the criminally insane. (While Scully and Mulder are in the asylum, someone in the background says over and over, "Forty-two, forty-two, forty-two.") The agents must go into Eve 6's cell with flashlights because Eve can't tolerate much light. She tells them that she and seven other Eves were bred, or cloned, with extra chromosomes, giving them heightened strength and intelligence—as well as psychosis.

Kendrick kidnaps the second eight-year-old, as she did the first, planning to reunite all the Eves. But the little girls poison Kendrick. Scully and Mulder come on the scene at that point, not yet realizing

<SCULLYISM>

Are you able to breathe?

the girls are murderers.

While in the care of Scully, the two girls try to poison the agents, but Mulder discovers the attempt just in time. The girls are put away with Eve 6. At the end, Eve 8 enters Litchfield. Obviously, the story isn't over.

Best line: The girls, "We just knew."

Plot problem: When Eve 8 enters the prison, she is not handed a flashlight, although the importance of a flashlight has been stressed to Scully and Mulder.

Fire

An old flame of Mulder's enlists his aid in protecting a visiting member of Parliament, which lights a small spark of jealousy in Scully. It seems that members of Parliament are being set on fire by a pyrokinetic serial killer.

Scully learns that the villain, L'ively, was employed by two of his victims and is currently in the United States, working on the grounds of the visiting diplomat's home.

L'ively soon tries to kill his man. While Mulder struggles to overcome a fear of fire to rescue the diplomat's children, Scully challenges L'ively. But he bursts into flames.

The episode ends with Scully's narrating that, as L'ively is recuperating from severe burns, authorities are unsure how to incarcerate him.

To look for: Scully typing on the computer is a repeat of a shot used in "Squeeze." And, when on the phone requesting a fax, Scully looks at her watch, which has both analog and digital display. The digital reads 4:22:ll, and the analog reads 5:05. Five seconds later, the analog reads 4:50.

Beyond the Sea

This is the first episode focused on the human side of Dana Scully. In many ways, it sets how she is viewed throughout the rest of the series.

Scully's father dies from an unexpected massive heart attack. Scully stands with her family as her father's ashes are scattered on Lake Michigan's rainy surface and the gay song "Beyond the Sea" plays. She wants some assurance from her mother that her father learned to be proud of her, but Maggie Scully can't give her what she needs.

Returning to work soon after, Scully joins Mulder in investigating the kidnappings of two college students, about which a death-row inmate claims to have psychic information. Scully is baited when Boggs, the inmate, promises her a message from her dead father. He's testing her, and we see a side of Scully never seen before.

Mulder is concerned about his partner. The two agents do some heavy arguing.

Boggs provides cryptic clues to finding the kidnapped teens. When Scully is in her car at an intersection, she suddenly sees the signs, enabling her to find the kidnapper's hideout.

The FBI enter the hideout, and Mulder is wounded by the kidnapper, who gets away with one of the kidnapped teens.

Scully returns to Boggs with more reason than ever to believe his psychic claims. The interaction between them is brilliant. (It's also Chris Carter's version of *The Silence of the Lambs*.) Boggs presses her for a deal: a message from her father for a stay of execution.

Scully must decide if visions he presents to her are true or the by-product of her grief. The nonbeliever who always demands concrete evidence must question her convictions. She lies to Boggs saying she will make the deal, and he tells her where to find the remaining kidnapped teenager. She rescues her.

Scully forgoes Boggs's execution—and any possible message from her father—to visit Mulder in the hospital instead. She admits to him that she is "afraid to believe."

A scary and well-written plot, designed to produce an outstanding performance from Gillian. She superbly portrays someone who desperately wants to believe, making Scully sincere and true to character.

To look for: The shots of Scully driving alternate between the things she sees and shots of her. In one, she is suddenly reversed: her hair is parted on the wrong side, her rearview mirror is to her left, and the car lights behind her are over her left shoulder. It looks as if she's driving a car with the steering wheel on the right side.

Genderbender

Scully and Mulder investigate the deaths of three women and two men who died while having sex, possibly from induced heart attacks. Clues lead the agents to a strange cult known as the Kindred. (Are they alien colonists?) One member, Andrew, tells Scully about Brother Martin, who left "to become one of you." Andrew tries to seduce Scully, who is grateful for Mulder's intervention.

The agents aren't certain if the murderer they're looking for is male or female. They track the suspect to a motel where, after a struggle, they apprehend the character—still not knowing "its" gender.

This story could be smutty; instead, it is thought-provoking and disturbing. One of Mark Snow's creepiest soundtracks backs it up.

To look for: After the head Kindred woman asks the agents not to interfere, Mulder leads Scully away. From one camera angle, he leads her by the hand. From a different angle, he has his arm around her. Then back to the first angle, and he's again leading her by the hand.

Lazarus

During a stakeout, Scully shoots bank robber Warren Dupré. Scully's former lover and fellow agent, Jack Willis, is seriously wounded.

Willis miraculously returns from death. Though Mulder believes that Willis "is not who he is," Scully stands by Willis during his trauma.

Willis informs Scully that he knows where Dupré's wife/accomplice is hiding. They go to Lula Dupré's, but once there, Willis turns on Scully. The persona of the dead Dupré has possessed him. Scully tries to bring back Willis by reminding him of the birth date they share—February 23. Three years ago, when they were lovers, she gave him a "Happy 35th" watch.

Willis (and Dupré) soon die again, this time of Willis's diabetes, about which Dupré didn't know.

Lula, far from grieving, demands from the FBI $1 million for Scully. But the feds hone in on Scully's location and save her.

Plot problem: Although the Duprés use Scully's cellular phone and Mulder says they can't trace the call, the Cigarette-Smoking Man finds Mulder using a cellular in the later "Anasazi" episode.

Young at Heart

The atmosphere of this one is eerie, in part because the actor playing the convict owns one of the creepiest voices ever heard.

Reggie Purdue warns Mulder that a convict who swore vengeance against Mulder is on the loose. But the guy is recorded as dead. Investigation reveals that the death certificate was signed by a Dr. Ridley, whose license was revoked for regeneration experiments on humans.

Ridley tells Scully that his work was financed by the government.

Meanwhile, the regenerated convict has decided that the best way to hurt Mulder is to hurt Scully. His fingerprints are discovered on Scully's answering machine. He follows her to a cello recital, where agents stake him out.

When the convict shoots Scully, she's protected by a bulletproof vest. He in turn is shot—but will he regenerate and be heard from again?

To look for: In the opera building, a full-body shot of Mulder shows him wearing a black earphone. Switch to the next close-up, however, and he isn't.

E.B.E.

Looking for more information concerning multiple UFO sightings, Scully accompanies Mulder to visit a group of conspiracy watchdogs known as the Lone Gunmen. Listening to Mulder's ideas, one of the men says, "That's what we like about you Mulder. You're weirder than us."

Deep Throat both helps and hinders as Scully and Mulder find themselves tracking an unmarked

<SCULLYISM>

Lots and lots of files.

truck that might be carrying the occupant of a crashed UFO. Scully and Mulder follow the truck.

Following the truck in Washington State, they see a blinding light, similar to those reported in alien encounters. In the aftermath, the truck has been turned completely around in the road and is facing them.

Chasing the truck's driver, they breach a government power plant, but are soon halted by MP security. Deep Throat is on hand to explain that our government is in a secret pact with others to exterminate any extraterrestrial biological entities (E.B.E.s). He also tells about a secret conference after the Roswell incident in 1947, which included East and West Germany.

Best line: Deep Throat's, "A shark dies if it stops swimming. Don't stop swimming, Mr. Mulder."

Plot problem: The two German states were not founded until 1949.

To look for: When Scully is about to get into the truck that she and Mulder chased down, in one camera shot she has her flashlight; in the next she doesn't and has moved one step forward.

Miracle Man

When people who have touched a faith healer start dying inexplicably, Scully and Mulder probe the Miracle Ministry. They find Samuel, the healer, in a bar, believing his gift is tainted.

This time it's Scully who solves the mystery and gets the limelight. As Samuel is brought to trial, the courtroom fills with locusts that she exposes as fake. The agents discover the locust plague was in fact the work of a human.

Samuel is beaten to death in jail—but he's also seen walking out. Meanwhile, the agents trace the source of the locusts to a man Samuel saved from dying of severe burns. Horribly disfigured, the man is angry he was saved.

Scully is more skeptical toward religion than in other episodes. She and Mulder seem to share skeptic/believer characteristics in this one. He seems doubtful, and she seems almost believing, or at least accepting. They both suggest nonreligious, pro-science explanations. And they both show a sense of humor. It works well.

Gillian Anderson makes a rather thin Scully in this episode.

Best line: When Mulder first visits the healer's tent and says, "Wait, here's where they bring out Elvis."

Shapes

A scary and rewatchable installment.

Scully learns from Mulder that the very first X-file stemmed from events in a Southwestern werewolf case. Now a boy is wounded by a creature the boy's father shoots and kills. It turns out to be a Native American with wolflike fangs. The father is attacked next, on his porch. The son is found naked and unconscious nearby.

Scully takes the son to the hospital, and then for questioning. Tests reveal he has ingested his father's blood. The son transforms into the creature and attacks Scully. Of course, Mulder arrives just in time to shoot him.

Plot problem: When Scully is outside the bathroom, how can the wounded son of the murdered man hear her say she wants to take him to the hospital if she can't hear his loud howling? And why can't Mulder call Scully on the cellular immediately upon learning the results of the son's tests?

Darkness Falls

After thirty loggers vanish in a scenario similar to one from sixty years earlier, Scully and Mulder venture back to Washington State to investigate. In the woods, they find a huge cocoon containing the remains of a man. An ecoterrorist informs them of a nocturnal force that eats people alive.

Mechanical problems strand the agents, a ranger, and the logging company security officer accompanying them. The company man goes for help, but as it grows dark, a swarm of glowing green mites cocoon and devour him.

The ecoterrorist goes for help next. Scully chews out Mulder for trusting the man with their gasoline reserves. Predictably, their generator runs dry. In the sudden darkness, the mites swarm. Just in the time, the sun rises.

Later, Scully, Mulder, and the ranger are cocooned as they make a desperate attempt at escape. They are found, however, and treated. The bugs will be eradicated by a series of burns and pesticides.

Plot problems: When the generator runs out of gas, why didn't they just build a fire? And why weren't Scully, Mulder, and the ranger

< S C U L L Y I S M >

If this is monkey pee, you're on your own.

devoured when they were cocooned?

Tooms

"If you release Eugene Tooms, he will kill again!"

Though the FBI agents protest, Eugene Tooms, the liver-eating mutant killer of "Squeeze," is paroled. The parolee is provided with a room in a nice couple's home. While Scully attempts to find more evidence to lock him away forever, Mulder tries to prevent Tooms from obtaining the fifth and final liver he needs to go back into his nest for thirty years.

Scully is warned by Skinner and the Cigarette-Smoking Man against unorthodox investigative procedures, but acting on a tip from the retired investigator of the previous Tooms murders, she finds the body of a victim from sixty years ago.

When the agents also find the body of Tooms's psychiatrist—minus his liver—they know Tooms will return to his nest now. An edge-of-your-seat chase through a slimy crawl space ends with Mulder escaping Tooms who is crushed by the under workings of an escalator.

In the video release, Chris Carter tells that actor Doug Hutchinson insisted on doing this crawl-space scene in the buff. Being chased by a completely naked man seemed to stimulate David Duchovny to crawl *fast*. ("Tooms" may be Chris Carter's version of an old two-part *Kolchak* episode.)

When the Cigarette-Smoking Man is asked if he believes the report the agents turn in about Tooms, he says, "Of course I do."

Best line: Leaving the courtroom after his protest is ignored, Mulder says, "You think they would've taken me more seriously if I'd worn the gray suit?"

Born Again

This episode scares briefly but without leaving the disturbing images we expect from *The X-Files*.

Detective Barbala plummets to his death from the room where he was watching over a lost little girl. Scully and Mulder begin an investigation of eight-year-old Michelle, turning up evidence that may solve a case just one year older than she is.

Michelle is the reincarnation of a detective taking vengeance on those who murdered her in her last life.

She kills a second man, and confronts a third when Scully and Mulder stop her.

Plot problem: Scully and Mulder arrive in Buffalo with amazing speed! The locals are still taking pictures and examining the scene of Barbala's death when the two agents get there.

Roland

The X-files team investigates the death of two research scientists working on a jet engine. The evidence of advanced theoretical work seems to eliminate the possibility of a suspected, mentally handicapped janitor—until Scully and Mulder uncover his relationship to a third "dead" scientist.

The agents find that Roland, the janitor, had a twin, Grable, who was a scientist and whose head is cryogenically preserved. Maybe the twins share a psychic bond; maybe Grable is manipulating Roland to murder. The janitor runs when Scully and Mulder try to question him.

The music makes this episode dramatic and suspenseful.

Scully and Mulder coax Roland into shutting down the experimental engine before it sucks in and kills the last scientist.

The Erlenmeyer Flask

Scully takes a more central role in this season's-end cliff-hanger, and Gillian Anderson shows her capabilities.

When Deep Throat points out a news story about a fugitive who apparently drowned, Scully and Mulder cannot see what makes it out of the ordinary. Deep Throat says they've "never been closer to the truth." At his insistence, the agents investigate evidence of secret government experimentation with extraterrestrial DNA.

Soon, the evidence and those who have seen it begin to vanish. A man with a crew cut kills the experimenting doctor.

During the murder investigation, Scully takes an Erlenmeyer flask from the laboratory. She finds the doctor was cloning bacteria similar to plant cells but with a DNA not of this world.

When Mulder is taken hostage by the Crew-Cut Man, Deep Throat arranges to ransom him for Scully's samples of alien tissue.

In the chilling climax, Deep Throat is shot during the exchange. His last words are, "Trust no one."

Scully gets a call from Mulder two weeks later. "They're shutting us down, Scully." But Mulder vows to continue as long as "The truth is out there."

Best scene: Scully tells Mulder that for the first time she doesn't know what to believe.

Plot problems: When examining the laboratory after the murder, Scully should know better than to try to pet an animal research subject. And it seems she would have taken for her own study some of the samples of alien tissue before giving the rest up as ransom for Mulder.

SEASON TWO
Little Green Men

The investigation of the FBI X-files has officially ceased. Scully and Mulder have been reassigned. But an old friend gives Mulder a reason to keep his waning beliefs alive.

The man claims there is evidence of contact with extraterrestrials at a SETI program site in Puerto Rico.

When she meets him in sunny Miami, Scully learns of Mulder's plans to go to the site. (She's wearing a trench coat, despite the weather, because Gillian Anderson needed to hide her pregnancy.) Mulder has only twenty-four hours to get the evidence before a cover-up team of Blue Berets eradicates it—including anyone who knows about it.

Since Mulder goes without official permission, his FBI superiors want to find him. Concerned, Scully needs to get to him before someone else does. She looks for clues in his computer. Searching for the password for his secret computer files, she hits upon "trustno1."

Knowing she will find him, the Cigarette-Smoking Man and Skinner try to use her to track Mulder. As she heads to San Juan, however, she loses the agents tailing her.

Meanwhile, Mulder arrives at the jungle site. He circles a locked fence, then breaks into the padlocked SETI hut.

Scully arrives to find him unconscious after a "close encounter." Just as the Blue Berets arrive, the two agents make a run for it.

Later, Mulder discovers that the tapes he has made of the evidence at the site were wiped clean during his close encounter. He tells Scully that, although he no longer has the X-files, he still has his work—and her.

A lot of things happen in this episode, including a revamping of the story of Mulder's sister's abduction. In the pilot, Mulder and Samantha were in bed when Samantha was abducted. In this episode, the abduction occurred when they were playing a game of Stratego in the living room.

Best line: Mulder's "I live for Bach."

Plot problems: The SETI hut is padlocked when Mulder arrives, so why is there a guy still inside? And no locked fence stopped Scully—as it did Mulder—from parking conveniently outside the door of the hut.

To look for: Although Mulder's password for his secret files in his computer has eight digits, Scully types on nine keys before she hits the return key.

The Host

A great horror episode begins when a decomposed body is found floating in the brackish foam of Newark's sewers. Mulder is given the case. He thinks, because of the grossness of it, that he's being punished, and he tells Scully he's thinking about leaving the FBI.

However, Scully's autopsy of the body reveals a large parasitic worm.

Then a sewer worker is attacked and bitten, this time by a worm as big as a man.

> < S C U L L Y I S M >
>
> **There has got to be some explanation for this, Mulder.**

An anonymous tip informs Scully that the first victim was Russian. She reasons that the man-sized fluke might have been bred in the radioactive waste of Chernobyl.

The episode is full of yearning nostalgia between the separated Scully and Mulder. It also introduces X, Deep Throat's replacement. Combine these, the tension between Skinner and Mulder, and the gross monster, and you have an entertaining episode. Although the writers tried some repressed sexual tension, Gillian Anderson is *so* pregnant it just doesn't play.

To look for: Scully performs autopsy DP112148, Chris Carter's wife's initials and birthday. The body is John Doe number 101356, Chris's birth date.

Blood

A disappointingly Scully-less episode. A rash of killings in a small town brings Mulder to profile the murderers, a task made difficult by the fact that none of them had a history of violence. All died at the end of their berserk rages. The only clues are some destroyed electronics and an unknown organic substance.

Best lines: The elevator's readout, "Kill 'em all," and the readout on Mulder's phone, "All done. Bye bye."

Sleepless

Though Mulder is given a new partner, Alec Krycek, he "trusts no one" but Scully. She's been reassigned to her old position at Quantico. Still, she does what she can to help him with a case of a scientist's death.

The corpse suggests death from burning, but there was no fire.

The upshot is that soldiers were altered during the Vietnam War era, in an experiment to produce sleepless killing machines. But the lack of sleep brought on psychosis as well. One of the men has learned how to project hallucinations so potent they can kill by causing a man to believe he's burning to death.

This barely misses being one of the *worst* episodes.

To look for: Scully's students at Quantico industriously scribble notes, though their notebooks remain blank.

Duane Barry

Part one of three parts. Steve Railsback's acting makes this trilogy worth watching. An escapee from a mental hospital holds several travel agents hostage. Mulder is asked to help with negotiations, since Duane Barry claims to be a UFO abductee. Scully learns that Duane is an ex-FBI agent who was shot in the head, making him violent and delusional.

However, Mulder believes Duane's abduction story and is faced with the difficult choice of following standard hostage procedures or his own instincts. The best stories involve this type of dilemma: What's the right thing to do? But when Duane goes berserk, Mulder has no choice but to set the man up for waiting FBI snipers.

Once subdued, pieces of metal are discovered in Duane's body. On impulse, Scully scans a piece of this metal at the supermarket. The register goes nuts.

As Scully leaves a message about the metal on Mulder's answering machine, Barry crashes through her living room window. She screams into the phone for help.

To look for: Since Gillian was pregnant during the filming of this episode, they had her buying pickles and ice cream at the market.

Ascension

Part two of three, and a worthy follow-up to the previous episode. Returning home, Mulder hears Scully's message on his machine. Just then, a frantic Mrs. Scully visits. She's dreamed Dana was taken away.

Meanwhile, Duane, with a bound and gagged Scully in his trunk, drives toward a destination he will know only when he sees it. A patrolman pulls him over. Scully pounds for help on the trunk. Duane kills the alerted cop.

Mulder finds Duane's car too late. It's empty but for Scully's golden cross in the trunk. He finds Barry, however. The madman says "they" took Scully; he traded her for his own freedom.

<SCULLYISM>

What the hell are you trying to say?

Mulder revisits the site where Scully was taken. He looks into the sky with heartbreaking fear for his lost partner.

3

This episode was filmed while Gillian Anderson was on maternity leave.

Despite Scully's absence, Mulder finds the strength to continue his work on the recently reopened X-files. Mulder finds solace in the arms of another woman, played by David Duchovny's real-life girlfriend at the time, Perry Reeves. (What's that saying—when the cat's away . . . ?) He recognizes a killing as the work of a trio with a fetish for drinking blood.

Although the vampirism was intriguing, Mulder should have been looking for Scully rather than sleeping with another woman.

One Breath

The last part of the "Duane Barry"–"Ascension" trilogy. The introductory monologue of Scully's mother and the supporting photographs of Scully get this episode off to a terrific start. Mrs. Scully has had a headstone made for her daughter. Mulder insists it's too soon to give up on finding her. Indeed, Scully soon turns up in a Washington, D.C., hospital. Seeing her kept alive by machines, Mulder nearly goes mad. He even hands in his resignation. Skinner refuses it.

In dreamy sequences, Scully is shown in a small boat tenuously tethered to the dock of a lake. A mysterious Nurse Owens stands on the dock, encouraging her to hang on.

Meanwhile, the Lone Gunmen discover that Scully's DNA has been altered. In the hospital, a man steals a sample of her blood.

Dana's mother and sister decide to unplug her life-support systems. Mulder is against it, and Maggie Scully explains it's not easy for her either.

X tells Mulder that some men will ransack his apartment, and if he wants revenge for Scully's abduction, he should be waiting for them. As he waits, however, with his gun ready, Melissa calls from the hospital; Scully is weakening. Mulder gives up his chance at revenge to say good-bye.

But Scully rallies. Mulder's low-key joy is one of the best bits of acting David Duchovny has ever done. Even better is his breakdown upon realizing how near he came to acting in as cold-blooded a manner as those he despises.

Later, when Scully asks for Nurse Owens, she is told that there is no one by that name at the hospital.

One of the best-ever episodes. Though Scully lies unconscious through most of it, her presence saturates the story. Mulder's feelings for her are shown to go deeper than simple respect, deeper than friendship, perhaps even deeper than romantic love.

Note that every regular player was included in this script—Scully, Mulder, Skinner, the Cigarette-Smoking Man, Maggie, Melissa, and X.

Of course, the real reason Scully lay in a coma for this episode is by now common knowledge. Gillian Anderson was still recovering from the cesarean delivery of her daughter.

Best line: When Scully corrects Melissa for calling Mulder "Fox."

To look for: Mulder signs Scully's admission sheet with a signature different from that on his FBI card in the opening sequence.

Firewalker

Scully returns to action when scientists exploring a volcano's core send a distress signal. A videotape shows one of them dead. Scully and Mulder fly to the site to investigate evidence of a life-form able to live at incredible heat. One scientist grows violent, and dust bursts from his throat. Scully identifies the dust as a spore, which must have been inhaled and grown to maturity in the man's body.

When another scientist is overtaken by the spore, she handcuffs herself to Scully. Scully manages to evade the bursting spore by shutting the woman away in a chamber.

Plot problem: Surely Scully must have inhaled at least some of that puff of spore flying out through the crack in the door.

Red Museum

An episode of pure camp humor.

The X-files team is called when missing Wisconsin teens begin to reappear, wandering in their underwear, hysterical with fear. The phrase "He is one" is scrawled on their backs. The sheriff suspects the local vegetarian cult of harassing the meat eaters.

The ever-skeptical Scully and her believing partner are led by a town resident to a farm where they see growth hormones being used on cattle. Is there a link between the hormones and the recent violence?

A Dr. Larsen, who has treated the abductees with vitamin shots since their childhood, turns up dead with a briefcase full of money. Scully links him to the conspiracy. The Crew-Cut Man appears to kill a man injecting cattle. He in turn is killed by the sheriff.

The agents learn that a landlord has been abducting the kids because he believes that Larsen's "vitamins" made monsters of them. The vitamins are really alien DNA, the same featured in "The Erlenmeyer Flask."

To look for: As Scully and Mulder eat dinner, Mulder goes out to see what some kids are yelling at. He removes his napkin once, then again as he's walking.

Excelsius Dei

Scully's feelings come out whenever there's a situation of sexual assault. She and Mulder investigate after a nurse in a convalescent home is raped and battered by an unseen force. The home is full of unrest. A doctor has been experimenting on the Alzheimer's patients with a drug called Deprenyl, which increases acetylcholine levels.

But an orderly has also been treating the patients, with mushrooms.

A patient is choked to death by an unseen hand. Another patient, named Stan, seems to be involved.

In their hotel, Scully finds Mulder watching graphic porno movies, which he says are "definitely not his." Yeah, right.

They return to the home in time to see an orderly hurled out a window by an invisible attacker. Stan is present.

A bathroom floods, with Mulder in it. Scully saves him.

Mulder's conclusion is that some spirit of a dead patient has been unleashed.

Plot problem: Scully says that elevated acetylcholine levels can cause psychosis, but that's true only at very high levels.

To look for: The light from a large window that isn't supposed to be there is reflected on the bathroom wall.

Aubrey

In a dream, a pregnant policewoman experiences the memory of a serial killing. Later, she unearths the body of an FBI agent sent to investigate the killing nearly fifty years ago. Scully travels with Mulder to Aubrey, Missouri, to investigate.

When the killer strikes again, they work with the woman detective to find his identity. They discover he's an old and feeble man.

They also discover that one of his earlier victims survived. His rape left her pregnant, but she gave the baby up. The policewoman is the granddaughter of the killer—and through genetic memory is murdering as he did. The episode ends with her under watch after attempting to kill herself and her unborn child.

To look for: First, when Scully and Mulder are in the office talking, Scully reads a file. Several times, she flips a page over, but when we see her from Mulder's point of view, the page isn't turned.

Second, when Scully is riding in the car with Mulder, they pull to the side of the road. As soon as they stop, Scully heads for a house.

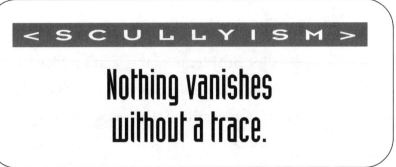

< S C U L L Y I S M >

Nothing vanishes without a trace.

Mulder puts the car in park, turns it off, unbuckles his seat belt, gets out, and goes around the car—yet gets to the house before Scully.

Irresistible

This is a realistic, suspenseful, even terrifying episode. There's some real character depth expressed when Scully and Mulder aren't chained to their stock roles of skeptic and crackpot. It also marks progress in the relationship between the agents.

A Minnesota agent claims that a female corpse, unearthed and mutilated, is the work of aliens. Mulder believes otherwise, and is vindicated when a similarly mutilated prostitute is found. Donnie, a mortuary worker, is the murderer. He's arrested trying to capture another woman.

Scully, meanwhile, has a nightmare relating to the case. She returns to Washington to talk to her counselor—the episode's best scene. Back in Minneapolis, Donnie is released after a cell mate gives him Scully's name. He runs her off the road and takes her captive.

During a ritual bath, Scully pushes Donnie into the bathtub. Mulder breaks in with reinforcements. Scully cries on his shoulder.

Scully has an especially nice closing monologue.

Plot problems: Scully and Mulder look over an opened grave in the rain, and though it seems they should cover the grave to keep evidence from washing away, they don't. Too, in the scene where Donnie captures Scully, she could have easily shot him. Finally, how did Mulder know where she was to rescue her?

Die Hand Die Verletzt

The occult makes for some scary subject matter in this episode.

When Scully and Mulder are called to look into the matter of a boy found dead with his heart and eyes removed, the town's Satan worshipers (the Parent-Teacher Committee) attempt to hide their tracks. They fear that the dead boy and his friends, while playing at occult rituals, have brought them all a little closer to Satan than they really wanted.

Again, Scully leads most of the investigative work. She and Mulder are told stories involving Satan worshipers in the town. Scully dismisses the idea, until she sees toads fall from the sky and water draining backward. Mulder tells her that the town's modern witches aren't responsible for what the agents are experiencing.

A girl, Shannon, reveals horrific stories of Satanic rituals that involved her and her little sister. Mulder goes after her stepfather. But the town's newest teacher sends Mulder a fake call saying Scully is in trouble, and Mulder leaves the stepfather handcuffed to a basement railing. Later, the agents find the man reduced to bones, apparently eaten and digested by a snake.

The Parent-Teacher Committee plans to sacrifice the agents to save themselves from the "presence" brought by the boys' naive play. But one member, possessed by the dead stepfather, turns a shotgun on the knife-wielding new teacher, then on himself.

The message, "Good-bye. It's been nice working with you," is found written on the dead teacher's chalkboard.

The ending is something of a cop-out: Scully and Mulder are saved at the last minute by someone else. Too, they draw their conclusions almost as fast as they get their handcuffs off.

Best lines: Mulder's, "You really do watch The Learning Channel."(This episode aired right before the miniseries Gillian hosted on TLC.) And Scully's, "Mulder, toads just fell from the sky."

Plot problems: Though Scully knew that it would take longer than forty-five minutes for a big snake to digest and spit out a human, she doesn't seem to note that it takes much longer than forty-five minutes for a grown girl to bleed to death from slashed wrists. Also, she and Mulder break the law when they look to see who checked out the witch-craft book from the library.

Fresh Bones

No aliens and no monsters in this one. Scully and Mulder are called in by a grieving wife, fearful of voodoo, to investigate the deaths of two soldiers at a Haitian refugee camp. Scully discovers that the corpse of the latest victim, a Private McAlpin, has been replaced by the body of a dog. Later, the agents find a figure walking in the road. It's McAlpin.

<SCULLYISM>

Nature didn't create this thing—we did.

A soldier tells them that a refugee named Bauvais warned the camp's colonel that he would take his men home even if they weren't given permission, resulting in Bauvais's being beaten to death. This soldier soon turns up dead, too. The agents find out that he and McAlpin had filed complaints about the colonel.

The colonel performs voodoo over Bauvais's coffin. Bauvais rises, and blows a powder on the colonel, killing him.

As the agents leave, the colonel is shown shut in his own coffin, alive and screaming.

An enjoyable episode.

Colony

A not too exciting episode. In part one of two, Scully brings Mulder into the emergency room at the hospital, warning the doctors that his hypothermia is what is keeping him alive. The story is told in flashback.

Scully and Mulder learn that several identical-looking abortion doctors have been killed by the pilot of a crashed airship of mysterious origin. A field agent wounds and arrests the pilot, but a virus in the culprit's green blood coagulates the agent's blood, killing him. As the X-files team arrives, the culprit transforms to look like the field agent and escapes.

Mulder's abducted sister, Samantha, returns with a story about cloned alien parents (the abortion doctors) being chased by an alien bounty hunter (the pilot).

Scully races the bounty hunter to find more of the identical doctors, whom she places in protective custody.

Mulder shows up at her hotel room door. She lets him in, then she gets a phone call—from the real Mulder.

Plot problems: You can't help but wonder how the alien chasing Scully knew what bus she'd take. And the producers seem to have a recurring problem with telephones: Why didn't Mulder call Scully on her cellular when he reached her answering machine? And when Scully calls to check the V-mail, she takes off after the first message, not bothering with the rest.

To look for: While Scully talks to the ER doctor, Mulder wears no oxygen mask, though he does in the shots before and after.

End Game

Part two of two. When Scully realizes the man in her room is not Mulder, she pulls her gun on him. But the bounty hunter overpowers her and takes her as a hostage to trade for Samantha Mulder.

Mulder arranges a trap. He'll only pretend to give up his recently returned sister in exchange for his partner. But the trap goes awry, and though Scully is released, Samantha is recaptured.

Scully asks Skinner for help when Mulder follows the alien to his ship in the arctic. She also contacts X, but is refused any information.

Skinner and X battle, and soon Skinner is at Scully's door with information to help her.

She finds Mulder on the Arctic ice where he was left to die of the virus in the bounty hunter's blood. She keeps him cold so the virus can't take effect on him.

Best line: As Mulder recovers, he tells Scully, "I found something I thought maybe I'd lost: faith to keep looking."

Many historic events are related to the "universe" of the show through past-life regression tapes made by a hypnotized Mulder; but Scully, Mulder, and Cancer Man traveling through time together? Cheesy.

Fearful Symmetry

Scully and Mulder check out the local zoo, which has never had a successful animal birth. It seems an escaped elephant may have done some fatal damage downtown. Or was the damage due to an invisible force?

An unsmiling Scully-and-partner meet with zookeepers and the head of an animal-rights group. Scully believes the animal-rights group is behind the trouble. She tails a member who breaks into the zoo. He's killed by a tiger freed from its cage by a flash of light.

Questioning a gorilla who understands sign language, the agents find the animal is afraid of bright light.

Scully's autopsy on an elephant reveals it was pregnant, though it was never mated. The same is true of the dead tiger.

Gillian and David bring this script to life—but we could have done without Scully climbing around inside that poor elephant.

Dod Kalm

Scully sneaks into a military hospital to see a survivor of an abandoned U.S. Navy Destroyer. He looks ninety years old, though he's only twenty-eight.

The agents board the destroyer in Norway, where ships have disappeared in Bermuda Triangle–like circumstances. On board, they find mummified corpses. Their own boat is stolen, leaving them stranded. They discover the captain, a drunk who soon dies of old age, though he is only thirty-five.

The agents themselves age thirty years. As Scully writes in her journal that it's the ship's contaminated water that's causing the problem, Mulder loses consciousness.

They awaken in a hospital, rescued by Navy Seals—and the information in Scully's log.

Plot problem: The abandoned-ship setting was good, but according to Norwegian sources, the foreign dialogue was badly delivered. Right words, wrong syntax.

Humbug

The Gillian-Anderson-eats-a-bug episode. Scully and Mulder must separate the paranormal from the abnormal when they explore a long-standing series of ritualistic killings that match no known patterns.

When the alligator-man of a circus sideshow is killed by a mysterious creature, the agents travel to Florida to investigate. They check into a trailer park in a town of sideshow performers—people like Lanny, whose twin brother, Leonard, grows out of his side. Nothing here is what it seems.

The agents discover that Lanny's twin has disjoined himself and is looking for another brother. They chase the creature, but he escapes.

Leonard attacks the Conundrum, who eats anything. When the agents arrive, the Conundrum, unhurt, is rubbing his stomach, digesting. He doesn't feel well. "Probably something I ate."

An unusual case, with quirky, somewhat endearing characters; Scully doing what she does best; and a surprise ending. Mulder's wry humor gets some opportunities as well.

He and Scully were both wrong in their deductions about this one. A strength of this series is that the heroes aren't superbeings who know everything, but can be surprised like any normal person. Also, Gillian's fans appreciate a woman who not only can perform autopsies without getting queasy and can use a gun with dexterity and skill, but who will even eat crickets.

To look for: Scully pretends to eat the bug that Gillian really did eat—or at least chew. Although she takes the bug with her right hand, when she shows Mulder, it's in her left hand.

The Calusari

Scully and Mulder go to a small town to investigate a death Mulder believes is ghost-related. Speaking with the parents of a murdered boy, Scully notices the Romanian grandmother drawing a swastika on the hand of another son, Charlie.

Later the grandmother dies, and Charlie cries that his stillborn twin brother, Michael, killed her.

Scully pursues the ghost, Michael, while Mulder gets help from the Calusari—three suited Romanians who do exorcisms. As Mulder holds

Charlie down, the Calusari perform their ritual. Just as Michael is about to kill Scully by smashing her into walls, the ritual ends, and Michael vanishes.

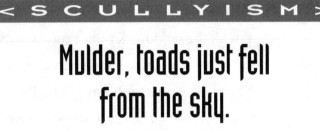

< S C U L L Y I S M >

Mulder, toads just fell from the sky.

Frightening.

To look for: A big yellow toy fish that faces the play-schoolroom door. Later, when Charlie suffers an attack and Scully and Mulder rush into the room, the yellow fish's tail faces the door.

F. Emasculata

The X-files team is called in to aid a manhunt for a prison-escapee. They realize something unusual is up when they see a quarantine in effect. A Dr. Osborne tells Scully that ten men have died from a highly contagious and deadly disease. Scully sees the bodies being incinerated. The two escapees may be carrying the contagion.

Scully discovers that a pig's leg was sent to a convict by Pinck Pharmaceuticals. When Dr. Osborne dies of infection, there is no one to corroborate her theory that the pharmaceutical company sent the infection to the penitentiary to test its deadliness. Scully argues to Mulder that they can't go public with their suspicions because they lack proof.

To look for: When Scully reaches with her tweezers to pick a bug out of a pustule on a dead prisoner, she doesn't have her mask on. When she looks at the bug in the next shot, she does have it on. And by the way, for truly aseptic purposes, shouldn't she be wearing a surgical suit?

Soft Light

Despite all the pseudoscientific rationalization for this episode's phenomenon, the laws of physics and plain common sense make it ridiculous.

Scully gives an ex-student, Kelly Ryan, a hand investigating a series of disappearances. They consider the possibility of spontaneous human-combustion. But then police approach dark-matter experimenter Dr. Chester Banton and, upon touching his shadow, are vaporized. Banton can be apprehended only when the lights are off. His shadow is a black hole, vaporizing anything it touches.

Later, the agents are shown a bogus video of Dr. Banton disappearing in a particle accelerator. In reality, he's been taken prisoner by X and others in the government for secret study.

Plot problems: Among other flaws, when Banton's former partner tells Scully about their experiments with quarks, gluons, and mesons, she states that nobody knows for certain if they exist. *Every* physicist knows they do. If she's supposed to have a degree in physics herself, she should also know that changing the matter of the average person into energy would produce enough power to blast a large chunk out of the planet.

To look for: When Mulder sits in the train station, Scully seems to miraculously appear from behind a column.

Our Town

Scully and Mulder are sent to Dudley, Arkansas, to find a missing poultry inspector. The slogan outside the processing plant reads Good People—Good Food.

Scully is bound and gagged by chicken-plant founder, George Chaco, who takes her to a ritual attended by many of the townsfolk, who just happen to be cannibals.

Chaco is beheaded after an argument with the plant manager who prepares to do the same to Scully. Mulder comes to her rescue.

One of the most disgusting episodes, which makes it memorable.

To look for: When Scully does an autopsy, we see her looking at a slide of the woman's brain. But how did she obtain brain matter without cutting into the cranium?

Anasazi

Part one of three episodes that deal with an MJ DAT tape.

The trust between Scully and Mulder is sorely tested when he begins to act strangely. For instance, Scully is shot at while visiting his apartment. She's worried. And she's told that they are both in danger of losing their jobs.

Meanwhile, the Lone Gunmen give Mulder pirated documents detailing the defense department's UFO files. They are written in Navajo, which was used as a secret-code language during World War II.

The Cigarette-Smoking Man quickly takes action to retrieve the files, while Scully investigates Mulder's abnormal behavior. She discovers the water in his apartment is drugged, which explains his outbursts of violence.

Mulder's father is visited by the Cigarette-Smoking Man to discuss the missing files. Mulder visits his father too, but the evil Krycek

<SCULLYISM>

I'm surprised she didn't call Oprah as soon as she got off the phone with the police.

shoots the elder man before he can talk to his son. In shock, Mulder calls Scully, his father's blood all over his hands. She warns him that his recent behavior might make him look guilty of the murder.

Mulder goes to Scully's and collapses. On awakening, he finds both Scully and his gun missing.

Later, he is about to kill Krycek when Scully intervenes. She shoots Mulder in the shoulder to bring him down, then takes him to New Mexico to recover. Meanwhile Scully goes to a Navajo woman to have the file translated.

Mulder wakes after thirty-six hours. Scully urges him to find out more about the files because her name is a recent entry.

Later, Mulder witnesses the destruction of alien corpses in a train boxcar. "What have they done?" he asks.

Plot problem: Scully is a petite woman and Mulder's a six-foot-tall man, so how does she move him when he's unconscious?

To look for: When Scully and Mulder examine the coded files in their FBI basement office, he doesn't have on the suit coat he wore in the previous scene with Skinner. Too, when Mulder is shown in shock over his murdered father, his hands are bloody; but when he gets to Scully's apartment, they are clean. And in the Navajo Nation office, as Scully stands to leave, the reflection of a boom mike moves in a picture frame on the wall.

Excellent performances by Gillian and David, and an excellent example of character-drama writing.

But, Scully's name still isn't on the door to the basement office, even after two years of being teamed with Mulder. Maybe when she gets her name up there, Gillian Anderson will get the same pay as David Duchovny.

SEASON THREE
The Blessing Way

In this second of three parts the transitions between the separate plot elements do not flow smoothly. Scully is taken to the smoldering boxcar in the desert. She doesn't find any sign of Mulder. Driving away, she is stopped by a helicopter. Troops pour out. A soldier searches her, while another checks the trunk of her car. They take her printed copy of the pirated UFO files.

While a wounded Mulder bakes in the motionless noon back in the desert, Scully, in Washington, D.C., is suspended from work for direct disobedience. After a confrontation with Skinner, she goes to Mulder's desk, where she discovers the digital tape is missing.

After leaving FBI headquarters, she realizes a computer chip has been implanted in her neck. She cuts a hypnotherapy session short upon remembering where the chip was implanted—in a train-car laboratory.

Back in the desert, Mulder is rescued by a Navajo.

At Mulder's father's funeral, Scully meets the Well-Manicured Man, a member of the Cigarette-Smoking Man's cabal. He warns her she will be killed, either at home or by someone she trusts.

Scully finds herself at a loss as to what her next step should be and turns to her family for support. Her sister, Melissa, decides to visit her. Scully, anxious about the Well-Manicured Man's warning, calls back to tell her to wait, but there is no answer.

Scully tries to intercept Melissa, but meets Skinner, who demands she get in his car. Not trusting him, they go to Mulder's apartment, where Scully pulls her gun on her superior.

Melissa is mistakenly gunned down at Scully's apartment by Krycek and another man.

At Mulder's, Skinner tells Scully he has the digital tape. Footsteps approach the door, distracting Scully. Skinner draws his weapon, resulting in a standoff.

Again, we are left hanging. Will Scully at last be forced to face her abduction experience, owing to discovery of that implanted chip?

To look for: Although a bullet intended for Mulder grazed Scully's forehead in season two's final cliff-hanger "Anasazi," no mark appears in this season's opener, a continuation of that same story.

Paper Clip

Part three of three episodes. With Scully and Skinner deadlocked at gunpoint, Mulder enters, shocking the two, who had thought he was dead. The X-files team forces Skinner to put down his weapon. Skinner insists he must hold onto the disputed tape, reminding them that it's the only leverage they've got against the cabal.

Reunited, the agents take a photo of a group of men, including Mulder's father, to the Lone Gunmen, who direct the agents to another man in the photo, Victor Klemper. Klemper is a scientist from Nazi Germany, pardoned through an operation called Paper Clip.

Scully now learns that her sister has been shot.

Klemper directs the agents to an abandoned mine in West Virginia, which might also lead to their deaths, for he then informs the Well-Manicured Man of what he's done.

At the mine, Scully and Mulder find a vault containing a labyrinth of files, the medical records of millions of people. Scully and Samantha Mulder both have files there. Samantha's file was originally Mulder's; her name is pasted over his.

The lights go out. Mulder sees a craft hovering overhead. Strange beings rush past Scully (the relevance of which is uncertain). A hit squad arrives, but the agents escape through a back door.

Skinner meets them. He wants to help them by trading the tape for their lives.

Stopping at the hospital to visit the wounded Melissa, Skinner is beaten up by Krycek and two others.

Scully and Mulder return to Klemper's, but find the Well-Manicured Man. He tells them of alien-human genetic experiments.

Sadly, Scully's sister dies, and the agents pledge to search for answers. Scully has heard the truth, now she wants to know *why*.

Excellent performances from Gillian, David, Mitch Pileggi, and Floyd "Red Crow" Westerman, who plays the Navajo code-breaker Albert Hosteen, Mulder's rescuer in the desert.

Plot problems: First, Skinner claims he couldn't copy or print out the encrypted data downloaded by the hacker, but Scully and Mulder gave copies to the Navajo code talker and the woman in the Washington office. Did they copy them out by hand? Unlikely.

Second, if Hosteen knows what the files say, why doesn't he tell Scully and Mulder?

Third, in the early part of this episode, when Scully and Mulder escape from the mine through the back entrance, it is an unguarded, claptrap, wooden door. Too convenient, considering they needed a code to get in the front.

To look for: Mulder drives a blue car similar to Scully's to the mine. Presumably, they left it there during their escape out the back. Then they go to a diner—how? Later still, Skinner takes them home in his car. What happened to their car?

D.P.O.

Scully and Mulder travel to Oklahoma to investigate after a teenager's heart is "cooked in his chest." Five people have been struck by lightning in this rural town. The investigation leads to the only person to have survived a lightning strike, Darren Oswald. Scully and Mulder pinpoint him as the prime suspect. Able to call down and control lightning, he fries several more people before he's finally apprehended by the agents.

A refreshing change from the previous sagalike episodes. It seemed closer to reality; and the music was great.

Clyde Bruckman's Final Repose

< S C U L L Y I S M >

I'm back, and I'm not going anywhere.

The X-files agents track a serial killer preying on fortune-tellers. The feds talk to Clyde Bruckman, who found the latest victim. Scully is suspicious of Bruckman.

But the killer makes it known he is targeting Bruckman, so the agents hide him in a hotel room.

Scully and Mulder reenact a scene Bruckman has envisioned, in which Mulder is murdered, but before the killer can strike, Scully fatally shoots him.

Back at Bruckman's apartment, the agents find Bruckman has committed suicide, no longer able to deal with his "gift."

Lots of jokes, perhaps because this episode was originally aired in 1995 on Chris Carter's birthday, October 13, which was a Friday that year. Actor Peter Boyle found the right note between tragedy and comedy as the insurance salesman, Bruckman. Writer Darin Morgan's script was impressive.

Best lines: Mulder's, "That's . . . a miss." And Clyde's, "You expect me to believe that's a real name?"

To look for: When Clyde plays poker with Scully, he holds a "dead man's hand," all aces and eights.

Also, Clyde predicts that Scully will never die, which later becomes important to fans worried about their heroine's well-being.

The List

Scully and Mulder are called into service when a death-row guard turns up dead a few days after prisoner Neech Manley is executed. Manley made a vow to return from the grave and kill his former enemies. Fear of the dead man's retribution has everyone scrambling to learn if they are on his list of five victims.

Scully believes the death of the guard to be the work of inmates and guards, while Mulder wonders if Manley really has returned. The agents find Manley's executioner dead, his body riddled with fly maggots. Unknown to the agents, each of the murders is precluded by a fly, which becomes Manley.

Scully and Mulder, with backups, raid the house of Manley's widow, now the lover of one of the executed man's guards. They find the woman fatally shot by her lover, who claims he saw Manley in the house.

Though there have been only four deaths, the agents depart, still pondering the possibilities of reincarnation.

A fly later appears in the prison warden's car. The vehicle crashes full speed into a tree.

This episode has many of the series' great qualities—the dark environments, the evil characters, and an ending that leaves everyone wondering—but its main strength is pure gore.

2Shy

Scully and Mulder investigate the death of a woman found partially digested by a gelatinous fluid.

As Scully prepares to examine a more recent victim, she is shocked to discover the body has melted into an oozing liquid. The mucus covering it is a digestive liquid used by the killer to devour the woman's fat.

Monitoring an on-line Internet service, the agents track down a woman named Ellen, who has arranged to date the suspected killer. When they find her, she's already fallen victim to him. Scully gives medical aid. The killer attacks Scully—who beats the living daylights out of him. Ellen also rouses, grabs Scully's gun, and shoots the man.

Plot problem: Scully pulls the goo out of a woman's mouth barehanded but doesn't get burned—or digested—by it. Also, at one point, she and Mulder touch hydrochloric acid, which should immediately eat through their skin.

To look for: Although Scully seems always at a loss for words in this episode, when a sexist detective hassles her for being assigned to the case, her icy stare is memorable.

The Walk

Several suicide attempts involving a phantom soldier in a military hospital interest Mulder. General Callahan, the commanding officer is uncooperative. Scully thinks he's covering up the insanity of his men.

After the agents leave him, however, Callahan sees the "phantom soldier." He later cooperates with Scully and Mulder when his son and wife are murdered.

An attendant blames Rappo, an unlikely suspect since he's a quadruple amputee. When the phantom attacks Mulder, the attendant

<SCULLYISM>

Do you have a theory?

suffocates the sleeping Rappo, and the phantom disappears forever. Was it a case of astral projection?

There are moments of fun between Scully and Mulder, but for the most part, a general lack of humor marred this episode.

Oubliette

In this above-average episode, the X-files team investigates the abduction of a girl, Amy Jacobs. Scully, along with police, suspect the involvement of a former victim of the kidnapper, Lucy. Scully won't listen to Mulder's theory that there may be a psychic link between Lucy and the kidnapper.

Somewhat cold toward her partner, she carries on her investigation without him. When she tries to arrest Lucy, however, the woman runs away.

Together, the agents track the kidnapper to a forest hideout. They find only Lucy hiding in the basement cell. This confirms Scully's suspicions, while Mulder remains adamant about the psychic link.

They leave Lucy in custody of another officer as they try to rescue Amy, whom Lucy insists the kidnapper is about to drown. They save the girl, and Scully gives Mulder credit for his instincts. But Lucy meanwhile begins to choke up water, and dies of drowning.

Plot problems: Scully's medical knowledge fails her twice in this episode, once when Mulder claims that one in five people has blood type B-positive (it's 6.6 percent), and once when she lets him stop CPR on the drowned person after just a few seconds.

Also, Scully's reaction to Mulder's involvement with Lucy was almost word-for-word like the one in "Conduit." Although in that case it was justified, the script writers' doubting-Scully syndrome grows tiresome. Mulder's emotions do sometimes interfere with his professionalism, but after two years of working so closely with him, Scully should be allowed to admit that he sometimes intuits things others wouldn't consider—or even want to.

Too, although the exchanges between Scully and Mulder are intense enough, their relationship leaves something wanting in this episode. The chemistry is missing.

Nisei

Part one of two episodes that open a new world of plot possibilities.

A mail-order videotape of an alien autopsy spawns a complicated investigation when Scully and Mulder find the distributor murdered in his home, apparently by a high-ranking Japanese diplomat.

Four Japanese nationals were murdered several weeks before, and someone must have identified the four doctors who performed the autopsies—because that person has been murdered, too.

As Scully follows up individual leads, the one strong point of this episode's plot occurs. She finds herself recognized by complete strangers who "remember" her as an abductee. They too had been abducted—and each had an implant removed from her neck. Scully learns that the implant is a chip used to track and record and even to alter memory.

While Mulder tries to find out more about the origin of the video, X meets with Scully and warns her that a suspicious train Mulder has found is bound for trouble. She must make sure he doesn't board it.

She does warn him, but he jumps onto the train anyway, believing an alien body is aboard.

731

Part two of two. This episode has a new tag line, Apology is Policy.

Mulder is trapped on the train with a Japanese scientist and a man sent to kill him, while Scully takes X's advice and investigates deeper into the implant removed from her neck. She traces it to a West Virginia address. There, she finds frightened survivors of a leper colony. One man relates their ordeal, which involved a Dr. Yama, human experimentation, and death squads. As he shows her mass graves, helicopters descend. Scully is apprehended, and the leper is shot.

Meanwhile, Mulder is locked in a boxcar by a National Safety Association agent, who says there is a time bomb aboard. (Although this is a formula used in too many episodes—one of the agents falls victim to the perpetrator, leaving the other to perform the rescue—at least it's not Scully who needs rescuing this time.)

Scully is taken to a friend of the Well-Manicured Man. He confirms the human atrocities at the lepers' colony before showing her a train car identical to Mulder's—identical also to the one she recalls from hypnosis therapy. It was here that she was "worked on" when she was abducted. The implication is that beings previously perceived as aliens could be the result of government experiments.

She calls Mulder's cellular and discovers his plight. He believes that someone will save him because of the important alien cargo. Scully argues that the cargo is a human experiment subject, and further, that if the train blows up, it will spread a deadly disease. With only minutes to spare, the agents discover the exit code to Mulder's car. As he opens the door, he is blindsided and beaten by the NSA agent. X rescues him.

In this episode, we're left to wonder if Scully is being duped. She witnesses many unexplainable things for which "they" offer an explanation and let her see evidence, but are they simply molding her to continue her disbelief of alien visitations? Now both Scully and Mulder know what they've seen. So which is right? He seems to reject her proof out of hand. And she does buy this wrap-up of her abduction a little too fast. Yet there's a logic problem if she remains skeptical of Mulder while accepting the story of the cabal member—a story that doesn't explain what she learned at the lepers' colony.

The scene in which Agent Pendrell hides his feelings for Scully is cringingly awful. And the scenes in the lepers' colony are ridiculous. Would Scully casually walk and chat with a man whose face is peeling off, acting as if there's nothing wrong?

Revelations

An episode for those who never thought Scully could be a believer or Mulder could be a skeptic. And one that ranks right up there with "Beyond the Sea" as Scully-intensive. Our FBI agent's character is further developed as she and her partner investigate the murder of an evangelist who faked the miracle of stigmata, spontaneously appearing wounds like those of the crucified Christ. The agents are alerted to a young boy, Kevin, in Ohio. He may be the next choice of a fanatic who has, so far, murdered eleven other stigmatics.

The boy asks Scully if she is the one sent to protect him.

Although Mulder says, rather bitterly, "I pray for miracles every day," he thinks this case is one of "fanatics behaving fanatically, using religion as an excuse." Scully's religious convictions force her, however, to look for a spiritual—i.e., irrational—explanation.

This disagreement could have given rise to a fascinating exploration of the spiritual dynamic between Scully and Mulder—why she can believe only in God, and he can believe in everything but God—but the producers missed their chance. We're left to think for ourselves: Could it be that all along she's been his touchstone? When he climbs into in a bubble of wild hypothesizing, it's always Scully who keeps him firmly anchored to the ground. Therefore, it could be unsettling for him to see her blowing bubbles too.

Or perhaps divine possibilities are just different from extreme possibilities.

Whatever the reason, Scully's faith in things unseen and uncertain saves the day in this episode. When a gardener is killed trying to protect Kevin, she detects the "odor of sanctity" on the man's body. Mulder is almost sarcastic when he asks if she thinks she's the one sent to save Kevin. In fact, she *is* beginning to believe she's been chosen. She even vows to protect Kevin.

The agents take the boy to their hotel, where Scully's maternal instincts surface. Mulder puts on a puppy-dog face and jokes that Scully never draws his bath. But she ignores the peace offering.

The killer snatches Kevin from the bathroom. How Scully tracks them to a recycling plant through a "full circle" reference is questionable. (She looks at a trash can, sees the recycle symbol, and figures it out.)

<SCULLYISM>

You're stronger than this. Fight him, Mulder!

She confronts the killer, who jumps with Kevin into a paper shredder. The boy is miraculously unhurt.

As Kevin returns to a children's shelter, Scully sees his stigmata wounds have healed. But he tells her she will see him again.

A final scene in a church confessional allows Scully to deliver one of the most memorable lines of the series: "I'm afraid that God is speaking, but that no one's listening."

Obviously, we're to conclude that Scully doesn't wear a crucifix merely for its jewelry value. So why didn't she believe in Samuel's powers in "Miracle Man"?

To look for: When Scully has the school nurse take Kevin's temperature orally, she does so with a rectal thermometer. Too, Scully mistakenly claims that a reference made to St. Ignatius is from the Bible. Also, although the stigmata appear on both sides of Kevin's hands, there are bandages only on the backs of his hands when Scully rescues him.

Mulder is shown in an unsympathetic light in this episode, and the two kidnappings of one child make it less than believable. The use of the recycling-symbol is even worse. This series is full of leaps of imagination, but not on Scully's part. Still, the reversed roles serve to differentiate "Revelations" from previous episodes.

War of the Coprophages

Scully tells Mulder that his theory about the deaths of residents of Miller's Grove, Massachusetts, is a load of crap. Several people have been attacked by killer cockroaches, and Mulder believes a war of worlds is going on between an alien invasion of roaches and earth roaches.

Scully finds a fuel researcher who has a license to import dung. She thinks it more likely that the exotic dung is responsible for the roach infestation.

In their next phone conversation, Mulder says he wants to confess something to her. He's met someone, an attractive female scientist. Her name is Bambi.

"Her name is Bambi?"

Scully arrives in Miller's Grove ASAP. She tries to get a map in a mini-mart. When some candy spills on the floor, everyone screams and runs, thinking the rolling candies are roaches.

Scully catches up with Mulder and the woman entomologist with whom he's become involved. The look on Scully's face when she meets Dr. Bambi Bernbaum is classic.

The cellular phone conversations with Scully, the scene in the mini-mart, and Scully's rival, Dr. Bambi, make this experiment with pure camp very funny. We also have guest characters parodying Scully and Mulder, the slow build of another of Mulder's theories, and Gillian Anderson's wonderfully deadpan delivery of Scully's best-ever lines. Darin Morgan wrote a tender, sincere, emotional scene as Mulder put the moves on Bambi. But for once, "Spooky" has met someone weirder than himself—and he doesn't quite know what to do with her. He turns to Scully for midnight comfort and to bare his soul. And does she enjoy giving him advice?

In an accident, the "crap" factory explodes and the two agents are covered with imported dung. A suitable ending.

Scully's reaction to a love interest for Mulder is engaging; but never fear, she still gets to play the skeptic—three times.

To look for: Scully reading *Breakfast at Tiffany's*. Interestingly, David Duchovny missed an answer having to do with this book on the game show *Jeopardy*. It cost him the match.

This was writer Darin Morgan's third outlandish episode, including "Humbug" and "Clyde Bruckman's Final Repose." He seems particularly adept at capturing both the sexual chemistry and humor between Scully and Mulder.

Syzygy

The X-files team answers a local detective's call for help when several small-town teens are found dead and rumors of a Satanic cult abound. Scully thinks it's a matter for the police, not the FBI. While she and Mulder bicker, he flirts heavily with Detective Angela White.

Attending the funeral of the latest victim, the agents witness the coffin burst into flames while two teenage girls, Margi and Terri, look on holding hands.

The unusual level of tension between Scully and Mulder is also apparent in the townsfolk. Is it because of fear and anger, or is it written in the stars, as an astrologer claims? An alignment of the moon and the

< S C U L L Y I S M >

There's something up there, Mulder.

sun might be drawing out the negative and evil inner parts of all the various characters.

The relationship trouble between the agents is portrayed fabulously. Finally we see the petty sides of Scully and Mulder. Her skepticism becomes outright hostility, and Mulder is just plain obnoxious. Some of the insults they throw at each other are brutal. They argue like an old married couple over things like road directions and stop signs. Seeing Scully smoke and Mulder get drunk are special pluses.

Hey, it's all a parody—and it's not as if they're never going to chase aliens again.

Scully interrupts Angela's seduction of Mulder with news of the latest death. Margi and Terri have killed a girl to get her boyfriend, then they kill the boyfriend. Each girl implicates the other in separate questioning. When the agents bring them together, objects fly and guns go off. The agents wrestle the girls into a storage room and lock the door, restoring peace.

Best lines: Scully gets extra points for, "I bet she's not even blonde." Mulder's, "I didn't know if your tiny feet would reach the pedals," is a close second.

Chris Carter wrote this episode. Was it an experiment with Scully and Mulder's interactions? They all took risks. It was refreshing to see Gillian and David put such a different spin on their roles.

This episode is no typical thriller, and the plot is certainly not of the highest caliber, but it was a nice change. It was about time Scully and Mulder had a fight.

Grotesque

It's back to business for Scully and Mulder. They are asked to help Mulder's former mentor, Bill Patterson. Bill's three-year murder investigation has come to a close with the arrest of a gargoyle artist who claimed to be possessed by an evil force. But the murders continue.

Scully suspects a copycat killer, but Mulder thinks there may be something to the artist's belief that he was possessed.

The upshot is that Patterson is now possessed and doing the killing.

Scully doesn't play a big part in this episode. She worries a lot about Mulder's fragile mental state. And she stumbles into a situation with no clue as to what is going on, causing a near disaster by blinding Mulder with her flashlight while he's holding Patterson at gunpoint. It seems the writers could have done more with her than this.

Piper Maru

Part one of two, this episode is named after Gillian's daughter.

Scully and Mulder are alerted when members of the crew of the *Piper Maru* are admitted to a hospital in San Francisco. The crewmen suffer from radiation burns. And at least one of them brought something oily and menacing back with him.

Scully's thoughts return to her murdered sister as she visits the naval base where she grew up. She questions an old neighbor about the undersea location where the salvagers on the *Piper Maru* had been diving to the remains of the *Talypus*, a sunken World War II ship.

Skinner, meanwhile, is ordered to close the investigation of Melissa Scully's murder. Then he is shot in a seemingly random act of violence.

The exchange between Scully and Skinner in their scene together lacks any emotional subtlety. Gillian Anderson's acting is unusually weak and one-dimensional. Otherwise, the episode is one to keep you on the edge of your seat.

Apocrypha

Part two of two. While Skinner is taken from surgery after being shot, he whispers to Scully that he knows the man who shot him. Scully discovers the gunman is the same one who shot her sister. She spearheads the investigation of the killer in hopes of resolving Melissa's murder case.

Scully saves Skinner's life from his would-be assassin, Luis Cardinal.

Meanwhile, Agent Krycek has become the depository for the mysterious oily menace the salvagers brought back from sea. Krycek escapes Mulder's pursuit, and ends up in an abandoned missile silo. The oil, an alien being, pours out of his eyes and mouth and soaks into its hidden spacecraft.

Plot problem: When Scully's looking for a male with B-positive blood, she says she learned his blood-type from a waitress's description. Since when can waitresses tell a blood type? More than that, this particular plotline needs some grand denouement, where our protagonists emerge older and wiser and start off in some new direction. In other words, enough is enough.

It was nice, however, to see Scully lose her cool when she saves Skinner. Gillian Anderson deserves acclaim for this scene.

Pusher

The cold war between our intrepid agents starting in "War of the Coprophages" and continuing in "Syzygy" is over, and the spark and repartee have returned. Scully and Mulder are asked to help bring in a killer who makes his crimes look like suicide. The man has the ability to control others with his mind, and since he wants a challenge, he leaves clues for Scully and Mulder to follow.

When the agents and the local police search his apartment, he calls and proceeds to talk the local detective to death—literally.

Pusher is a villain equal to the darkest of the X-files cases, with a cruel and egotistical nature and a completely brutal way of murdering. Can the agents bring this one in? The plot becomes as hypnotic as its villain.

The agents' arguments with each another are perfectly balanced—not too aggressive—as they spar with sharp intellectual weapons. Scully becomes more accepting of Mulder's theory of telekinesis when they explain the situation to Skinner. The villain, unfortunately, picks up on their allegiance, and uses it against them. The horror gradually builds, until Scully and Mulder find themselves in mortal danger.

In a climactic scene, Pusher tries to make Mulder play Russian roulette with Scully. Mulder whimpers a heartfelt "Scully" as he points the gun at her, and their whole relationship can be seen in his expression. As always, Scully brings him back from the edge. "You're stronger than this. Fight him, Mulder!" Torn between wanting to pull the trigger and trying to hold back, he resists Pusher's commands long enough for her to set off a fire alarm, which breaks Pusher's control of his mind.

The final explanations given for Pusher's actions leave a lot of doubt and confusion—typical of the best *X-Files* episodes.

In the closing sequences, the camera focuses on the two agents briefly holding hands. This episode epitomizes the chemistry that makes the show work so well. The appeal of the series isn't just UFOs and the paranormal. Much of it comes from the humanity that makes the main characters more than trigger-happy, badge-flashing stereotypes. An example is the scene in which Scully naps on Mulder's shoulder. He wakes her with a gentle caress of her face, teasing her fondly with, "I think you drooled on me."

Gillian's acting was superb. Do you know how difficult it is to look that beautiful while allowing only one perfect tear to fall slowly down your cheek?

Plot problems: Again there was an instance of Scully stopping CPR too quickly. And early in the episode, when she and Mulder try to intervene as the local detective is being talked to death, they are physically restrained by other police. Would local officers interfere with FBI agents that way?

Teso Dos Bichos

People involved in the excavation and display of an ancient South American shaman's remains begin to die in a bloody, unexplained way. An ancient curse is connected with the remains of the female *amaru*, but Scully wonders if it's not merely a case of political terrorism. A reclusive member of the original excavation team, Dr. Bilac, opposed the removal

of the bones. He has become something of a madman, but Scully finds him too preoccupied with a native hallucinogen to be a real suspect.

Finding toilets at the museum plugged with rats, Mulder says, "It's as if the rats were trying to escape something." The agents follow strange noises into a labyrinth of old steam tunnels. Scully discovers hundreds of stray cats turned bloodthirsty. They move to attack her, but she manages to escape through a steam vent.

The museum returns the corpse to its burial site.

Those hoping for interaction between Scully and Mulder or any character development will be disappointed in this one.

Hell Money

When a night watchman discovers a man being burned alive in a funeral home, Scully and Mulder investigate the deaths of Chinese immigrants in San Francisco. With the aid of a Cantonese-speaking detective, they chance upon clues that lead them to a game in which players bet their very lives.

In an autopsy, Scully discovers that a number of organs were removed from a body prior to death, causing suspicion of a black-market organ transplant business. They meet an old Chinese man, Hsin, whose daughter, Kim, is fatally ill. Hsin doesn't have the money for the operations Kim requires. He's uncooperative with the agents, but Mulder sees Detective Chao talking secretly with him. Tailing Chao, the agents are led to a concealed building where a grotesque lottery is taking place. Participants put up vital organs in a slim gamble for wealth. It's a fixed game, however.

Scully and Mulder arrest the surgeon behind it all, but he seems unconcerned.

This case doesn't really qualify as an X-file.

Jose Chung's "From Outer Space"

Scriptwriter Darin Morgan makes fun of Scully and Mulder once again, as Scully recounts a case of alien abduction for science fiction writer Jose Chung's next book. The episode contains occasionally hilarious exchanges between Scully and Mulder, and an especially great use of dry humor when Scully and Mulder act as Men in Black. (Scully can't quite get it right.)

The autopsy movie Chung shows Scully, *Dead Alien: Truth or Humbug*, recalls *Alien Autopsy: Fact or Fiction*, a real film.

This is a lark, full of absurd comedy and confusion, as in the scene when Scully performs an autopsy on the body of a supposed alien only to discover it's a U.S. Air Force pilot in a gray costume. The agents wonder if the military, in the guise of aliens, has been abducting people for tests.

In other places, Scully is proclaimed not female, and Mulder not human. In fact, Mulder is a potato-pie eating, bigfoot watching, ticking time bomb of insanity.

Gillian and David were good sports to do this, but parody can never take the place of episodes involving revealing moments between the agents intertwined with a fascinating and deceptive plot.

Best lines: Scully had them both: "You're a dead man!" and "Mulder, you're nuts!"

Avatar

Scully and Mulder come to the aid of Skinner when he wakes in bed with a dead prostitute. He half believes he may have killed the woman, but Scully and Mulder refuse to accept that. The X-files team makes it their mission to get to the bottom of things and clear their boss.

But they find that Skinner's marriage of seventeen years is breaking up, and that he's being treated by a psychiatrist for a sleep disorder that could be responsible for erratic, even violent, behavior. It seems the agents' attempt to clear him is instead piling up evidence against him.

They continue to dig, however, and uncover what appears to be a conspiracy to get rid of Skinner, which was initiated by the same men who had him shot—and who lurk behind the smoke of the Cancer Man.

An amazing episode, incorporating paranormal possibility and government conspiracy.

Quagmire

The agents investigate a series of deaths on a small lake famous for its resident monster. Big Blue is a legendary aquatic dinosaur similar to the Loch Ness monster. As people continue to die, Mulder presses to have the lake closed. Scully and the sheriff resist.

< S C U L L Y I S M >

No one does anything without a reason.

Scully is dragged by her partner down to the site in Georgia. "But did you have to bring . . ." Mulder pauses as the camera pans to the weirdest creature ever to appear on the series, "your dog?"

Venturing out at night in a boat, Scully and Mulder are stranded on a rock in the lake. Scully's ugly dog becomes a victim of the lake monster, and the agents spend a tense night of fear and confession before the sun rises to reveal that they're only a few feet from shore.

An environmentalist tells them the frog population in the area is dwindling rapidly. He is soon after attacked by an alligator. Mulder is disappointed; it seems a mere gator must be the killer beast.

However, a closing shot reveals Big Blue emerging unseen from the lake.

The scene on the rock was great. It's almost symbolic that the two otherwise sharp agents were "marooned" three feet from shore. But this intelligent scene was surrounded by an otherwise average script and pedestrian cinematography.

Scully really needs to be given some way to insist on investigation of normal suspects without sounding like a nag. And Mulder needs to stop blowing her off.

An ordinary episode with one extraordinary scene.

Wetwired

Scully and Mulder investigate a series of murders in a Maryland town. The main suspect is . . . television.

Scully discovers that all the murderers were avid tube watchers and recorders. After watching hours of the murderers' tapes herself, she becomes delusional, believing she sees Mulder meeting with the Cigarette-Smoking Man. She actually fires on her partner, causing Skinner to issue a search for her. She is considered armed and dangerous.

Mulder proposes subliminal messages are the real culprit. He tracks Scully to her mother's, where she again pulls her gun on him. Eventually, she relaxes, however, and is able to conquer the subliminal messages she's absorbed.

Talitha Cumi

Part one of two. Scully and Mulder investigate a man who disappeared after healing four victims of a shoot-out. As Scully searches files looking for this Jeremiah Smith, she finds there are many of them.

Mulder meanwhile receives word that his mother has been admitted to the hospital. She tells him of a secret hidden in an old family vacation home. There, he discovers she is more involved with the Cigarette-Smoking Man than she's let on.

Mulder faces off against X, and then against the alien bounty hunter, who is also on the trail of Jeremiah Smith. And Scully wonders what to believe.

The episode, and the season, come to a tense close.

SEASON FOUR
Herrenvolk

Part two of two. Mulder is busy in this episode, chasing Jeremiah Smith, eluding the alien bounty hunter, trying to save his mother, and learning the fate of his sister. Scully seems helpless to do much except embrace her sobbing partner in his hotel room.

While Jeremiah leads the chase to an eerie, isolated farm community, Scully turns to her science to analyze some data recovered from the miracle healer's files. Her investigations into his background at the Social Security Administration lead her to a disquieting conclusion. There are five of him, and they were cataloging the entire human population.

At the farm, Mulder finds clones of his sister, bred as worker drones. There are also some mysterious bees being bred. The bounty hunter arrives, and Mulder is helpless to save either Jeremiah or Samantha.

X is also murdered, after being identified as a traitor to the Cigarette-Smoking Man's cabal. But the bounty hunter is ordered to save Mrs. Mulder.

Best line: The Cigarette-Smoking Man's, "The fiercest enemy is the man who has nothing left to lose."

To look for: Scully wears her hair in a new style. Also, Agent Pendrell seems to fancy the fed fatale.

Unruhe

Scully is given the opponent in this one. A woman has a passport photo taken moments before she is kidnapped. Though she smiled for the camera, the photo emerges showing a terrified, screaming expression.

Scully struggles to find a logical explanation for what Mulder calls "psychic photography."

The not-so-warm-and-fuzzy repartee between the agents reminds us again of a long-married couple who care for each other but are also wise to each other's tricks. Scully's annoyance with Mulder's flippant remarks is perfect.

The kidnapped woman is found muttering the word *unruhe* just before she dies. She's been lobotomized. Scully dredges up her college German to translate: unrest.

Another woman is kidnapped and lobotomized. Scully realizes that the same construction company had job sites near each crime scene. While Mulder goes to Washington to have the psychic photos examined at the FBI labs, Scully follows up on her own lead. She questions German-speaking Gerry Schnauz as he walks on stilts for his work as a drywall sealer. Director Rob Bowman's visuals are next to perfection here, moody and effective, creating an unforgettable moment as the stilt-walking killer looms behind Scully while she speaks to Mulder on the phone. Her partner warns her that the killer has really long legs. Scully turns, mutters, "*Unruhe*," and Schnauz bolts.

Yet the special agent gets her man. Gillian's acting is impressive, but Pruitt Vince almost steals the show as a scary and fascinating villain. He portrays a man with a condition called nystagmus, which causes the eyes to jerk erratically and constantly.

As Scully fiercely interrogates the eyeball-challenged Schnauz, the look on her face is pure anger. Later, he escapes from jail. Mulder's blood runs cold when he finds photographs of Schnauz's next victim: Scully.

Scully is ambushed and sedated by the killer. Mulder's only hope of saving her is to study the clues in the photos, which are pictures of Schnauz's thoughts.

In captivity, Scully wakes to find herself bound into a dentist's chair. It's not quite a boilerplate case of helpless-female-in-distress, but close. Using halting German, she tries talking Schnauz out of his delusions; yet the wacky-eyeballed madman bends near her with the needlelike tool he uses for his lobotomies. He insists he must rid her of the *unruhe* that is tormenting her. He taps her forehead—where later in this season she will discover a cancer. Was this planned?

With hardly a moment to spare, a Mulder-saves-Scully scenario plays out. Scully's voice-over wraps it up.

Great focus on Scully. Anyone new to the show would have seen her as the real strength behind the partnership.

Home

Fans of the series have to be open-minded in order to enjoy this episode. Though residents in Home, Pennsylvania, treat each other like family, some of the townspeople take that idea a little too far.

A newborn is found buried in a shallow grave, and though the child's deformations show multiple genetic abnormalities, neither Scully nor Mulder believe this a matter for the X-files—until they learn more about Home's reclusive Peacock family. Apparently they have inbred into a feral, murderous clan.

Now that the family has dwindled down to three brothers, Scully and Mulder suspect the men have devised a grotesque plan to force some woman into involuntary pregnancy. The introspection by both

Scully and Mulder as they face this horrible possibility is a nice touch.

> < S C U L L Y I S M >
>
> # What the hell is this thing, Mulder?

While someone watches unseen, the agents explore the Peacock farm. They find the bloody evidence of a recent birth. That night, the local sheriff, Andy Taylor, and his wife are murdered. "They went caveman," Mulder says of the mutant Peacocks.

Scully and Mulder invade the Peacock farmhouse. When they discover the hiding place of the clan matriarch, they finally comprehend the appalling truth.

Scully and Mulder manage to kill two of the rampaging Peacocks. As Scully empties her magazine into one of them, all we can think is, *Reload, Scully, reload!*

This is clearly Chris Carter's version of *The Andy Griffith Show* meets *Deliverance.* Or was it *The Texas Chainsaw Massacre IV: The Inbreeding*? The writers at least added some great scenes between Scully and Mulder.

Worst scene: Where the mother says, "I'm ready."

Plot problems: Why didn't the agents arrest the three brothers out in broad daylight when they had the chance? And why did they go into the house without backup?

To look for: Scully and Mulder in the hog pen. She imitates, sotto voce, the piggy from the movie *Babe.* Also, note Mulder's constant "mother" comments to Scully. This thread will be taken up in future episodes.

Not one of the show's best efforts.

Teliko

Scully and Mulder combine folklore and science to solve the mysterious disappearances of African American men. But the real feature of this episode is Gillian Anderson's décolletage as she crawls through some ductwork.

The Center for Disease Control calls upon Scully to unravel the medical mystery of the men turning up dead—and without skin pigmentation. Scully discovers the victims' pituitary glands, which produce melanin and hormones, have been destroyed. Meanwhile, the killer strikes again.

The evidence leads Scully and Mulder to arrest a recent West African immigrant, Samuel Aboah. Tests reveal he has a bizarre and uncommon medical disorder: no pituitary gland.

A West African diplomat blames the mythical Teliko, evil spirits who suck the life and color out of their victims. A skeptical Scully hears out Mulder's theory that the Teliko are not ghostly entities, but members of a lost African clan who have survived over generations by hunting other humans and stealing what they themselves lack.

Aboah escapes and captures Mulder. As the killer crawls toward her, Scully must chase through ducts to save her partner's life.

The evidence in this show points most strongly to the probability that Chris Carter must have been too busy with *Millennium* this week to keep watch over his first brainchild. In his absence, this was writer Howard Gordon's version of *The Relic*.

Still, actor Carl Lumbly did a fine job, Mulder was at his wisecracking best, and Scully looked downright foxy.

Best scene: Scully trying to decipher Mulder's eye movements toward the killer.

Worst line: Mulder's reference to Scully's slicing-and-dicing.

Plot problems: Why didn't the Teliko blow a dart at Scully instead of leaping on her? And how did the agents know which construction site to visit?

To look for: The new informant, Marita Covarrubias, replacing Deep Throat's replacement, X. And oh yes, Agent Pendrell is seen hanging around Scully again.

The Field Where I Died

Scriptwriters Morgan and Wong were at their best with this one, though Scully takes a backseat in the plot. The agents interrogate a cult leader, Ephesian, and his six wives, one of whom seems to have multiple personality disorder. One of her personalities claims to have been Mulder's fiancée in a past life.

Scully, who has a hard enough time with MPD, let alone reincarnation, can't understand why Mulder is so obsessed with the woman's claim. Scully confronts him with his tendency to be destructive in his search for the truth. Since she's hustled into the background, however, we aren't given enough of her skepticism to balance out his easy beliefs.

Yet, the inclusion of Scully in Mulder's regression hypnosis is wonderful. Past-life links between them are revealed. She was a male friend in one life and was his father in Nazi-occupied Poland.

Kristen Cloke, acting the part of Melissa, was fantastic, showing real depth. Her character brought out the human side of Mulder and

<SCULLYISM>

I'm fine, Mulder.
Mulder, I'm fine.

the compassion in Scully.

Best scene: When Scully tells Mulder that even if she "knew for certain" she wouldn't change a day. Past-life loves or not, the real sparks fly when these two characters are together.

There is no clear explanation of why Scully and Mulder are assigned to this case, though that doesn't hurt the episode. There is a lot of character development for Scully and Mulder, no guns are fired and Scully isn't abducted.

Sanquinarium

Scully and Mulder test the credibility of a doctor's tale of being possessed as he performed a fatal liposuction. Scully logically assumes the doctor's sleeping-pill addiction caused a psychotic breakdown. She is dubious of Mulder's conclusion of black magic.

From there we have a repeating cycle of patients going under the scalpel of a psycho doctor and Scully and Mulder arriving on the scene minutes too late. The duo was completely ineffectual in this episode. In fact, would fewer deaths have occurred if they'd simply stayed out of it?

Nurse Waite worked at a clinic where ten years ago similar deaths occurred. Scully and Mulder search her house, finding a spooky den of guttering candles, incense, herbs, and witchy objects. But Waite is trying to protect patients against a Dr. Franklin, a black magician who practices human sacrifice. Found out, the villain slices off his own face and disappears.

Graphic violence. Poor continuity in the dialogue. Lack of background—medical, Wiccan, and otherwise. And the way Mulder keeps checking himself out in the mirror, we expect him to ask Scully if she thinks he could use a little improvement. Scully is professional and extremely competent, but seemingly without imagination in this one.

Musings of a Cigarette-Smoking Man

The Cigarette-Smoking Man listens via a bug in the Lone Gunmen's office as Frohike reveals to Scully and Mulder what *may* be the chilling, secret past of the Cigarette-Smoking Man. The agents, the heart and soul of *The X-Files*, don't make an appearance in this episode, save for a flashback of Scully's interview in the pilot.

Best lines: Both are the Cigarette-Smoking Man's. "Life is like a box of chocolates . . . a cheap, thoughtless, perfunctory gift that nobody ever asks for." And, "I could kill you any time. . . . But not today."

Though we see ne'er a perplexed Scully brow nor a handsome Mulder face, we do see into a character much wondered about. And the episode gives rise to more wondering. For instance, could CSM be Mulder's father? Recall the look of pride on CSM's face as, in the pilot scene, Scully describes what she knows of Mulder's reputation as a top FBI analyst. Is this Chris Carter's version of the Darth Vader–Luke Skywalker relationship in *Star Wars*?

Enthralling from beginning to end.

Paper Hearts

Scully plays a major part in this one, keeping both eyes open for Mulder in a "Beyond the Sea" role switch. Haunting dreams lead him to question what really happened to his sister. The dreams take him back to one of the first killers he profiled as an FBI agent.

Scully accompanies him to interview John Lee Roche in jail. Roche toys with them when he sees that Mulder is taking the case personally.

Mulder's next dream places Roche as the kidnapper of Samantha. When Roche won't answer questions about it, Mulder backhands him. Scully is afraid for her partner and tries to convince him the dreams are nothing but images from his subconscious. She is certain that Roche was not involved in Samantha's abduction and is only manipulating Mulder's emotions. She does not report that Mulder struck the prisoner.

Skinner is sympathetic when Mulder tells him his fears about Samantha, and he allows Mulder to interview Roche again—as long as Scully keeps an eye on him.

Meanwhile, the agents find the grave of another child killed by Roche before he was jailed. A frantic Mulder starts to dig. "Help me, Scully." The child is not Samantha. Mulder's face says exactly how lost he is.

Without notifying her or Skinner, Mulder releases Roche from jail and takes him to Mulder's childhood home in Martha's Vineyard. Scully is quick to give excuses for Mulder's actions, to no avail.

Mulder learns that Roche knows nothing about Samantha. With Scully and an irate Skinner on his trail, he plans to return Roche to jail the next morning. But Roche escapes—and abducts another child.

The agents apprehend the child-killer before he can commit another crime, and Mulder admits to Scully that she was right about his loss of objectivity.

Gillian Anderson gave a great performance of a human being responding to the pain of another.

Best scene: When Mulder asks Scully point-blank if she's ever believed that Samantha was abducted by aliens. Her look says it all.

Just as she gave up the chance to hear her father's last message in "Beyond the Sea," Mulder gives up the opportunity to find the body of one last child murdered by Roche, despite the remote possibility that it is Samantha.

Tunguska

Part one of two. The evil Krycek leads Scully and Mulder to intercept a Russian courier at the airport. They gain possession of an extraterrestrial rock. Inside is the same black oil seen in "Piper Maru." It congeals into tiny worms that penetrate the skin of the scientist who drills the rock open. The infected man stops breathing but is still alive.

Mulder goes to Tunguska, in Siberia, to investigate further. Unfortunately, he does not bother to get official permission, and he is imprisoned in a gulag. He is then scheduled for ominous tests with the black worms and an antidote called black cancer.

Best scene: Called in by a Congressional committee to report on her partner's whereabouts, Scully refuses to reveal his location. Hinting at conspiracies too involved to be believed, she's found in contempt of Congress.

Gillian Anderson sparkles in this episode.

Terma

Part two of two. The new tag line for this episode is *E pur si muove*, Italian for "And yet it moves."

For Scully and Agent Pendrell, the medical mystery of the black oil and worms starts to unravel when tests reveal a black worm-shaped organism attached to the pineal gland of the scientist infected in the last episode.

Later, at another Senate hearing, Scully is about to be charged with contempt again when Mulder appears, fresh from Siberia. This is too unrealistic, yet the plot moves on. His presence puts the attention back on the rock and the biotoxin.

The rock originally obtained at the airport was en route to a Dr. Chung-Sayre, the supervising physician at a nursing home in Boca Raton. Scully and Mulder travel to Florida to investigate, but arrive too late. Chung-Sayre infected his patients with the worms, but now he is dead. His killer, former KGB assassin Vassily Peskow, has injected all the patients with the black cancer, a serum that causes the worms to emerge from the poisoned person's body.

Still bent on finding a trace of evidence, Scully and Mulder go to New York to interview the head of a militia group who knows Krycek. Following a lead, they try to stop Krycek from hiding another rock in Terma, North Dakota.

Again, Peskow is one step ahead of Scully and Mulder. The agents arrive in Terma too late to prevent a fiery explosion that engulfs the last piece of evidence. They barely escape with their lives.

Their reports go from the Senate committee to Cancer Man, who puts them in the circular file.

Best line: "It feels good to put my arms around you," which refers to Mulder's nearly getting his arm lopped off during his adventures in Russia. Krycek did lose his arm. Now he's the one-armed man of *The X-Files*.

< S C U L L Y I S M >

Last time you were that engrossed, it turned out you were reading the adult video news.

Plot problems: Why does the courier dump the pouch when he has clearly escaped Scully and Mulder? And why is Mulder always running off on foolish, not to mention dangerous, crusades, leaving Scully to face all the heat at home? How does he get back to the U.S. so quickly?

El Mundo Gira

Scully and Mulder follow a trail of bodies left behind by what could be the legendary *chupacabra*. As they investigate the deaths, Mulder thinks that the events just prior to Maria Dorantes' death sound like Fortean events. Scully greets his thoughts with her usual skepticism. There was a yellow rain, which sounds less Fortean than just plain polluting. She can't tell much from a dead goat's corpse found at the site about the cause of death, however, and Maria's body is at the morgue.

Two brothers, Eladio and Soledad, were vying for Maria's affections. This lover's triangle convinces Scully that Eladio is the killer, since Soledad is missing.

Mulder talks Scully into examining Maria's remains. The state of the corpse shocks even Scully. Eladio denies killing his brother and Scully now believes his story. Her autopsy of Maria's body revealed that she succumbed to a massive fungal infection.

Just in time, Scully warns Mulder against touching or inhaling the lethal lichen, which is being affected by an enzyme from the yellow rain that accelerates fungal growth.

Scully, on the verge of losing patience with Mulder's theory of an alien enzyme, just wants him to find the man who is now spreading it—Eladio. Witnesses say little gray *chupacabras* descended to take him up in the sky with them.

Scully and Mulder do nothing much in this episode but chase the *chupacabra* and argue.

Kaddish

In a low-key episode, Scully and Mulder investigate Isaac Luria's death. The dead man's fiancée, Ariel, tells the agents that though she and Isaac received their wedding license, the marriage ceremony never took place. Scully and Mulder retrieve a store-surveillance tape from the VCR of a sixteen-year-old who participated, with two others, in the killing. The boy has been strangled.

Anti-Semitic pamphlets are tossed on the doorstep of the dead man's father-in-law. Mulder says that whoever printed the pamphlets probably knows who killed Isaac, and he and Scully interview neo-Nazi Curt Brunjes, owner of a copy shop. Brunjes claims the teenagers videotaped beating Isaac are unfamiliar.

One of the surviving teens eavesdrops as Scully tells Brunjes rumors that Isaac has risen from the grave to avenge his murder.

The teen and his friend dig up the dead man's coffin. One goes to their car for tools and returns to find his friend's body protruding from a mound of mud. Scully's explanation for this is weak, and even Mulder is without a ready explanation. They turn to Kenneth Ungar, a scholar from the Judaica Archives. He tells them about the golem, a creature created out of earth, with the Hebrew word *emet* inscribed on the back of its hand. To destroy the golem, the first letter *e* must be erased.

Brunjes is murdered. When the agents examine the surveillance camera's tape, they see a golem, whose physical features match Isaac Luria's. Ariel prepares to marry this look-alike Isaac. She expresses her love for Isaac, then wipes the letter *e* off his hand. The creature crumbles.

Though Scully took the lead in this investigation, both she and Mulder faded into the background. At least the love story was solid and refreshing.

Best line: Referring to the possibility of the Jewish man rising from the grave, Mulder says, "Why not? A Jew managed it two thousand years ago."

Unusual for an *X-File* episode was the sense of closure at the end. There seemed an acceptance by all that they were dealing with a supernatural being. No Scully-ish scientific alternative was given, and no loose strings were left hanging.

<SCULLYISM>

Mostly it makes me afraid that God is speaking, but no one is listening.

Never Again

The inevitable conflict between Scully's practicality and Mulder's obsession comes to a head. Mulder must take time off or lose several weeks' pay, and tension erupts as he tells Scully what cases need attention during his absence. She refuses to waste time on a Philadelphian that Mulder believes has UFO information. Scully feels she's lost sight of herself. Why, she doesn't even have her own desk, or her name on the door of the office they share.

Nevertheless, she decides to visit Mulder's Philadelphian. Technically, it's unlikely that an FBI agent would go into the field without a partner, but she does.

The man turns out to be an extortionist and his actions have nothing to do with the X-files. Scully follows him to a tattoo parlor, where she meets Ed, a handsome divorcé begging the tattoo artist to remove a recently acquired Betty Page—like design and the words Never Again. An undeniable chemistry develops between him and Scully, and Ed gives her his card.

Following a tense phone conversation with Mulder who is in Graceland, Scully sets up a date with Ed. After a few drinks, they return to the tattoo parlor, where she has the image of a snake eating its own tail tattooed on her back. Is this really our formally dressed FBI agent? The music during this scene is fantastic.

The pair returns to Ed's apartment. This courteous man suggests she spend the night because of the bad weather developing. Scully sees blood dripping from his tattoo and helps him off with his shirt. Intimacy develops, but before Ed can act, the Betty tattoo cries out—at least in his head—"Kiss her and she's dead!"

Scully sleeps on the couch.

Meanwhile, a peeved Mulder wonders where she is.

Morning. Ed goes out to get them breakfast. While he's gone, detectives roust Scully. A resident downstairs is missing, and blood was found in her apartment. The blood contained chemical abnormalities. Scully recognizes the same odd ingredients the tattoo artist used in the ink of her and Ed's tattoos.

When Ed returns, she reveals that the chemical now in their blood is an ergotic alkaloid that can produce dangerous hallucinations. Ed confides that he's been hearing his Betty tattoo taunt him. When he learns that Scully is an FBI agent, he attacks her. The cinematography during this struggle is incredible.

As Betty's voice urges him, he drags an unconscious Scully to the basement, intending to stuff her inside the incinerator. Scully regains consciousness in time to tell him to take control. He does, thrusting his arm in the incinerator to burn off the tattoo.

The air remains tense between Scully and Mulder. She reminds him that "Not everything revolves around you. This is my life." Mulder seems close to saying, "This is *our* life," but catches himself.

Even though this wasn't the best installment, it was about time Scully spoke up about being Mulder's grunt, gopher, and medical database. While she does valuable background work, he often chases lights in the sky and tilts at windmills. Scully has lost her sister and been abducted. A desk and a nameplate and a little respect aren't too much to ask in return.

Plot problem: Why isn't Scully affected by the ink?

To look for: The tattoo's voice is Jodie Foster's.

Leonard Betts

Scully and Mulder's next case involves the decapitated corpse of Leonard Betts, an ambulance driver, whose remains disappear from a hospital morgue. Scully theorizes that someone stole the body to sell it for parts. In a scene of terrific black comedy, she makes Mulder help her fish through the hospital's bio-disposal unit for the remains. They find Leonard's severed head, but the body remains missing.

As Scully performs an autopsy on the head, the eyes and mouth suddenly snap open. Very creepy. Tissue samples tell her that Leonard was riddled with cancer.

When Leonard's partner hears his voice over a radio, the woman is lured to a rendezvous, where Leonard kills her.

The agents search the trunk of the dead man's car and find bags filled with human cancer tumors. Mulder's theory is that Leonard is ingesting cancerous tissue to stay alive; he thinks they're dealing with someone who can regenerate himself.

A bearded man with a cancerous lung leaves a bar and is attacked. Afterward, the decapitated body of Leonard gives birth to a full-scale duplicate of his old self. Using the bearded man's car, Leonard attempts to run down Scully and Mulder, who dive for cover and open fire. The car explodes, incinerating Leonard. Or so Scully thinks. Mulder doesn't.

The agents stake out Leonard's mother's house. When an ambulance arrives, Scully and Mulder race inside. They find the woman clinging to life.

Scully accompanies her to the hospital, but Leonard, who has hitched a ride on the vehicle's roof, takes out the driver and pulls the ambulance into a parking lot. Wielding a scalpel, he tells Scully, "I'm sorry, but you have something I need." The look on her face is electrifying. However, in the resulting scuffle, she coolly defends herself with defibrillation pads.

Later that night, Scully wakes coughing from a nose bleed. She recalls Leonard's haunting words and that tap on her forehead in the "*Unruhe*" episode.

Best lines: Scully's "Mulder, I need your help. Your arms are longer." And Mulder's "We'll take a slice to go."

To look for: Scully has the tissue sample analyzed at the University of Maryland, College Park, but on the phone she tells Mulder that Leonard's mother lives "here in Pittsburgh," as in Pennsylvania.

Memento Mori

Every good show needs episodes that flesh out the characters. This one begins with a powerful scene of Scully's voice-over as she writes to Mulder in her journal. "I hope you will forgive me for not making the rest of the journey with you." This could be pure melodrama, but the depth of the episode that follows warrants it.

Under great strain, Scully shows Mulder an MRI X ray showing a cancerous mass on the wall between her sinus and cerebrum. Instead of requesting a leave of absence, she opts to contact the group of purported female abductees who recognized her as a fellow victim in "Oubliette." They have experienced similar symptoms after having implants removed from their necks.

With Mulder, Scully goes to the home of Betsy Hagopian in Allentown, only to learn that Betsy died two weeks earlier. While searching her house, the agents realize someone is downloading her computer files via a phone modem.

They apprehend Kurt Crawford, the man who downloaded the files. He claims he acted as he did so the government couldn't destroy the data. He points the X-files team to another abductee/cancer patient, Penny Northern.

Scully visits Penny in the hospital. The woman believes her doctor has isolated the cause of her cancer, and Scully agrees to let Dr. Scanlon begin treating her, as well. She checks into the hospital.

Mulder leaves Kurt to watch over Scully, but when Kurt is shot by the Gray-Haired Man, his body melts into a pool of green liquid. Unaware of this, Mulder and a clone of Kurt later access a computer terminal and download an ominous directory that contains Scully's name. Mulder's face is a picture of desperation as he hears the clock ticking for his partner. He hunts for the Cigarette-Smoking Man, willing to make any bargain to save Scully's life.

It's Skinner who finds the Smoking Man, however, and who strikes an awful bargain for Scully's life.

Mulder's hunt for research files pertaining to the disease-stricken female abductees leads him to discover that Dr. Scanlon is working for the wrong side. He also discovers, in a subterranean research lab, many vials of human ova. One has Scully's name on it. Apparently, all the eggs from her ovaries

<SCULLYISM>

What the hell is going on?

were "harvested" during her abduction. (Remember the scene in "Home," when Mulder says, "Scully, I've never thought of you as a mother before.") Some ova seem to have been used already for genetic experiments to produce creatures that are not fully human.

Mulder snatches the vial and also a disk with Scully's name on it. Then he instructs one of the Lone Gunmen, Byers, to find Scully and stop her treatments with Scanlon immediately. Discovered where he shouldn't be, Mulder is nearly killed by the Gray-Haired Man before he escapes the research facility.

When Mulder returns to the hospital, he finds Scully's bed empty. His face registers terror. And then relief when he learns his partner has been with Penny Northern, who has died. Mulder's voice wavers as he greets Scully.

Summoning her will, Scully tells her partner that she is going to fight her disease and continue her work. He clasps her face in both hands and gazes down at her with sad eyes, then gives her a protracted kiss on the forehead. A nice moment. He does not, however, tell her she is now barren, or about the pale-skinned, orange-haired clones bred from her ova.

The producers really got under the skins of Scully and Mulder in this episode. The scene in the hospital hallway, where the duo hold each other so tenderly, would have been inconceivable last season.

There is some mirroring here of "One Breath," from season two: Scully in a hospital bed while Mulder races to save her life. And we have to wonder how this new information fits with what's going on in Canada, with Samantha's clones, and with the black-cancer experiments in the Russian prison camp. How does it connect the alien destroyed in the train car, the mutant humans and dead leprosy victims, the bodies suspended in liquid in "The Erlenmeyer Flask," Scully's abduction, the bees in "Colony," the files in the caves . . . and so on and so forth?

Best scene: When Scully tells Mulder, "About what? What it feels to be dying of cancer? What it's like to know that there's nothing you can do about it?"

Best lines: Skinner's "There will always be another way." And Scully's "I'm fine. Quit staring at me, Mulder, I'm fine." Also Mulder's "The truth will save you. I think it will save both of us."

This had all the great *X-Files* components—conspiracies, aliens, the Gunmen (who had their best parts yet), suspenseful action, and Mulder-Scully interaction. And yes, the producers are finally admitting that Gillian Anderson is only five foot two while David Duchovny is six feet. In the hall scene, she leans her cheek against his chest, and he must bend to kiss her forehead. No high heels for once!

Great acting by Gillian Anderson. And Sheila Larkin gives a good, if short, performance as Scully's mom. Also good is Mitch Pileggi. Even William B. Davis is more evil than ever. David Duchovny's range of emotion is always phenomenal.

A four-hankie episode.

Unrequited

As General Benjamin Bloch speaks at the Vietnam Veteran's Memorial, Scully, Mulder, and other FBI agents feverishly hunt an armed man making his way through the crowd.

As the story unfolds in flashback, a general is murdered in his limousine. The driver has ties to a radical group, the Right Hand. The leader of this group sends the agents after Nathaniel Teager, liberated from a POW camp after twenty-five years. Scully suspects the Right Hand leader's story is a cover-up for an elaborately orchestrated conspiracy.

Meanwhile, a widow is told that her soldier-husband is still alive. She's given his dog tags to prove it. The woman later identifies Teager as the man who told her. Scully takes the woman to an ophthalmologist when her eye hemorrhages.

Another general is killed, this time inside the Pentagon, though FBI guards were placed to protect him. A security camera captured Teager's image passing through a metal detector, but the agents didn't see him. Teager can hide from a person's field of vision.

Who is to be Teager's next victim?

Back where we began, at the Vietnam Veteran's Memorial, Scully and Mulder race against the clock to stop the seemingly unstoppable assassin. General Bloch is rushed from the podium after the agents spot Teager in the crowd. But Mulder tackles Bloch seconds before gunshots flash from inside the General's limo. Agents kill the mad Teager.

Scully's defense of her perceptions and ideas are not strong enough in this episode. And the new informant, Marita, lacks any of X's and Deep Throat's menace. Since Mulder contacts her anyway, why doesn't

> **< S C U L L Y I S M >**
>
> # Mulder, that is science fiction.

he ask her about Scully's cancer? In fact, why are Scully, Mulder, and Skinner even on this case?

Plot problems: If the widow's vision is permanently scarred by Teager, why aren't Scully's and Mulder's affected? This blind-spot idea is pretty unrealistic.

Most important of all, *why aren't they trying to cure Scully's cancer?*

Tempus Fugit

Part one of two. At the Headless Woman's Pub, waiters sing "Happy Birthday" to Scully as Mulder pretends he didn't set up this surprise. Scully *is* surprised, since her partner hasn't remembered her birthday before. He even gives her a present, a key chain commemorating Apollo 11. Scully says, "You sure know how to make a girl feel special on her birthday." Great (and rare) smiles from our actors in this scene.

Before the celebration continues, they are approached by Sharon Graffia, who identifies herself as Max Fenig's sister. Max, the alien abductee in "Fallen Angel," had asked that the agents be contacted should any harm befall him, which it has. He was killed only hours earlier in a jetliner crash.

The agents attend a team meeting of the National Transportation Safety Board as cleanup at the crash site begins. The pilot's last words speak of an intercepting aircraft. Mulder spouts his UFO theories, and the NTS official says, "If we find Mr. Spock's phasor or some green goo, we'll know who to thank."

With the NTS team, the agents comb the crash site for possible clues. One man, Garret, secretly sprays the face and fingertips of a corpse with acid.

When a survivor is found, Scully concludes the man was exposed to extreme radiation. Also, the watches of the corpses show a nine-minute loss of time. From these clues, Mulder deducts that Max was abducted from the aircraft.

But he's wrong. Max's body is found in wreckage.

An air-traffic controller in the Air Force Reserves tells Scully, Mulder, and the NTS official that he was the last person to speak with Flight 549. He fears for his life, since his tower partner has already been murdered. As the agents drive the reservist away from the NTS headquarters, two automobiles give chase.

Scully and the reservist await a Federal Marshal at the Headless Woman's Pub. A shoot-out follows when the acid-spraying Garret suddenly appears and opens fire on the soldier. Scully shoots Garret in the leg. Agent Pendrell is shot in the crossfire.

As Mulder prepares to dive in a lake for the aircraft he believes collided with flight 549, causing it to crash, the man providing the boat and scuba gear asks Mulder what his experience is. Mulder answers, "I got a quarter out of the deep end once."

He soon gets more than a quarter; he sees a sunken UFO and the body of a gray alien.

Worst line: When Mulder tells Scully to take the reservist back to D.C., and she answers, "All by myself?" She redeems herself in the shoot-out, however.

Max

Part two of two. The wounded Garret escapes the Headless Woman's Pub, and Scully turns her attention to the wounded Agent Pendrell. Her nose begins to bleed, wordlessly reminding us of her cancer. Pendrell dies. Is this seemingly needless death meant to remind us that Scully and Mulder are up against some pretty ruthless people?

The reservist air-traffic controller meanwhile is placed under military arrest for the murder of his tower partner and for providing false testimony in a federal investigation.

Mulder is also arrested at the lake where he found the sunken UFO.

Scully meets with Sharon Graffia, Max's supposed sister. She has recently been abducted—again—and is now in a mental institution. Sharon has been in institutions before, which discredits her in Scully's eyes. The woman admits she stole an object from her aeronautical-engineer employer after Max insisted it could prove the existence of alien life. Max had one part of the object, Sharon had another part, and a third part is hidden. Sharon's evidence was taken from her during her recent abduction. Only the hidden part remains unconfiscated.

In Max's trailer, the agents find a tape in which Max says he has irrefutable proof that the military has salvaged alien technology to use in their own applications.

From clues, Mulder finds the third part of the object and boards a plane. He telephones Scully to meet him at Dulles airport. During his flight, his watch stops. The mysterious Garret, also aboard the plane, grabs Mulder's evidence. As time stops, Garret—with the evidence—is abducted right out of the airplane.

At Dulles, Mulder says Garret "caught a connecting flight."

The episode ends with a rather lengthy soliloquy by Scully as she figures out why Mulder gave her the key chain on her birthday. This is stilted and contrived, and seems only to serve as a setup for Mulder's one-liner, "I just thought it was a pretty cool key chain." Gillian Anderson cribbed this monologue as her acceptance speech for a best-actress award from the Screen Actor's Guild.

To look for: In part one, the watches Scully and Mulder find in the wreckage read 8:01, nine minutes *ahead* of the official crash time of 7:52. In part two, Mulder's watch is nine minutes *behind* Scully and Skinner's when he lands at Dulles.

And while we're on it, since watches are stopped during alien encounters, why aren't cellular phone calls?

"Max" was definitely a well-written and well-acted episode. The subtle references to Scully's cancer were adept. But we really didn't learn anything new. Nothing happened to complicate things further for Scully and Mulder. Meanwhile, Mulder still has the vial of Scully's ova and the disk with her name on it from "Memento Mori."

Synchrony

Scully and Mulder review the facts of a new case: Two cryogenic researchers, Jason Nichols and Lucas Menand, are approached by an elderly man as they argue on a city street. The man warns Lucas that he's about to be run over. A security guard stops the old man from harassing the researchers. Moments later, Lucas is struck by a bus.

The security guard is later found frozen to death. Scully concludes he was somehow exposed to chemical refrigerant.

Soon after, she and Mulder examine the frozen corpse of a Japanese cryogenic researcher, Dr. Yonechi.

The agents approach Jason's girlfriend, Lisa Ianelli, also a cryogenics researcher. With Lisa's help, Scully and a medical team successfully thaw Yonechi. But when his thawed body continues to heat, he bursts into flames.

It seems the technique used to freeze him depends on cold fusion, a technology of the future. Jason has come back from that future to stop cryogenic research breakthroughs that will allow time travel, the repercussions of which make life not worth living. (This is Chris Carter's version of *Back to the Future.*) Jason goes so far as to freeze his girlfriend, Lisa, then kill himself.

But Scully successfully resuscitates Lisa by putting her defrosted body into a cold tub to prevent the continuing upsurge of temperature. Recovered, Lisa gets back to work in her cryogenics lab.

Mulder tries to use Scully's own graduate thesis to make her understand his time travel theory in this episode. But the characters' banter seems stale, and the plot idea only partly fleshed out. The guest stars hold their own nicely, at least.

Small Potatoes

This episode touches upon the vulnerability of both Scully and Mulder. Word of five strange births is spread by newspaper tabloids, and the agents travel to Martinsburg to investigate. The five babies have been born with tails. Scully suggests the abnormalities may be due to groundwater contamination, or prescription drug interaction.

With the assistance of a federal health department doctor, she learns that each of the five children have the same father. Since the mothers all deny sleeping with anyone but their husbands, Scully next proposes the father may have used a tranquilizer to incapacitate and then rape them.

<SCULLYISM>

The truth is out there, but so are lies.

Investigation leads to a suspect, Eddie Van Blundht, a man born with a tail himself—though he had it removed. Scully and Mulder visit his house. There they find the mummified body of Eddie's father, a former circus performer billed as the Monkey Man. Scully's autopsy reveals an anomalous muscular structure beneath the surface of the elder Van Blundht's skin. If Eddy inherited the same trait, he can change his appearance to look like anyone . . . possibly the husbands of the mysteriously impregnated women.

On Eddie's trail, Mulder ends up locked in a remote hospital boiler room. Taking on his pursuer's looks, Eddie pretends to be Mulder. He returns to Washington with Scully, files a report with Skinner, and closes the case. Later, he shows up at Scully's apartment with a bottle of wine. After an evening of unusually relaxing and personal conversation, Scully tells him, "I really feel like I'm seeing a different side of you tonight." Eddie (as Mulder) leans close, preparing to kiss her. Scully's expression says, What on earth! . . . Just then, the real Mulder kicks in the front door.

Caught in such an intimate scenario, Scully's embarrassment is palpable. And Mulder too is chagrined.

This episode capitalizes on romantic hints between Scully and Mulder. Gillian Anderson's deadpan foil to Duchovny's whimsy is enjoyable. Scully not recognizing that Mulder isn't Mulder is a stretch for the imagination, but David Duchovny's dopey smile seen through Scully's peephole is a riot.

Darin Morgan does a great acting job. And the plot shows an outsider's reaction to Scully's and Mulder's lifestyles—Mulder's geek friends, kinky phone diversions, and chronic lack of sleep; and Scully's utter absorption with her work.

But keep the alcohol away from this woman. She lets loose every time she drinks. Remember "Never Again"?

Chris Carter has vowed not to let a romance between Scully and Mulder sidetrack the series, and this episode seems to have been a sop for the pro-romance viewers.

Best lines: Mulder's tease, "Scully, should we be picking out china patterns, or what?" And "Do you think the fall killed him?" when the age-hardened corpse of the Monkey Man falls from the attic. Eddie's complaint of "Where the hell do I sleep?" as he searches in vain for a bed in Mulder's apartment. Also, Scully reassuring Mulder, "I'm sure I don't need to tell you this, but you're not a loser." And his response: "But I'm no Eddie Van Blundht, either."

Best scenes: The autopsy, when Mulder carelessly breaks off the Monkey Man's tail and tries to reattach it to the corpse without Scully seeing. And when the new mother of a tailed baby insists she was impregnated by Luke Skywalker.

Plot problems: How did Eddie get from the baby-viewing area to the fertility clinic before Scully and Mulder? Why did Mulder not simply call Scully when he got out of the hospital boiler room?

And since Scully *still* doesn't have a desk in the basement office, where does she keep her stuff?

To look for: The umbrella scene. It's not raining. In fact, it's sunny.

Zero Sum

With Scully undergoing tests for the treatment of her cancer, Mulder asks for Skinner's help to solve a mystery concerning deaths due to deadly bees whose stings cause smallpox. This seemed a sort of filler episode, easy to watch, easy to forget. It could have been condensed into thirty minutes. It was a tie-in with the Jeremiah Smith ordeal and a good showcase for Mitch Pileggi as Skinner—in his underwear, no less (and no more). He's a fine actor. But Scully wasn't in it, and that's too bad.

Best scene: When Skinner takes several point-blank shots at the Cigarette-Smoking Man.

Plot problem: Where did all those bees go after they did their deadly deeds?

Elegy

A freaky plot in which Scully and Mulder track a series of murders that lead to a home for the mentally ill and a clue that makes no sense: Each victim had a warning from the dead, a ghost who left the message, "She is me."

The initial suspect is Harold, an autistic man who lives in the home and works in a bowling alley. Writer John Shiban's ending provides a

< S C U L L Y I S M >

Mulder, you're nuts.

rather weak surprise to wrap up this mystery—it's not Harold but his nurse who committed the murders. Scully has to fight for her life against this woman. She proves she's quite a scrapper.

Even more interesting than the deliciously spooky murder-and-ghosts plot is the fact that Scully sees one of the death-omen ghosts. First, we're reminded that she's dying (by yet another nosebleed; are there no other symptoms of this cancer?), and when she goes to the restroom to clean up, she faces something even more disturbing.

Typically, Scully has trouble believing what she saw. Instead, she doubts her own sanity. She tells her counselor that she feels an obligation to continue working because she doesn't want to disappoint Mulder. Then she admits the real reason. She needs Mulder's support. And "his passion."

The inclusion of this scene lifts the episode above the standard stand-alone X-file, since it deals with Scully's deepest emotions and her internal struggle to control them. This is a woman who has lost both her father and sister and hardly allowed a tear fall.

Toward the end, Scully admits to Mulder that she saw the warning ghost. Her partner sympathizes, knowing what the omen means, but he also gently scolds her, saying that if she isn't working with him she's working against him. Though she's admitted she needs his support, she only apologizes. Scully does not open to him in any way that could help her.

In a last heartbreaking scene, Scully slumps into her car—and sees in the back seat the ghost of the now dead Harold. Her facade of strength and independence cracks, and she weeps.

David Duchovny had a choice role in "Zero Sum"; this was Gillian Anderson's turn. She opened the door on the character of Scully a little wider. As for Chris Carter, he seems determined to make viewers wonder if Scully is going to be "killed off" the series. Was Clyde Bruckman wrong after all?

Best lines: Mulder's deeply concerned, "Oh, Scully." And Scully's more humorous line, when she holds up the *TV Guide*, "Do any of you recognize this man?"

Plot problems: Why did the nurse commit the murders? Why did she want Harold's medicines?

Also, nasal pharyngeal cancer usually spreads quickly, yet Scully seems able to go on week after week. If she isn't going to die, the time to reveal her cure is now.

To look for: Scully's expression as she puts on the pair of bowling shoes in the opening scene.

The theme of facing one's greatest fears resonates through this episode. The acting was subtle and superb, and the script offers all kinds of memorable moments.

Demons

This episode deals with Scully's relationship with Mulder, and warns her how far her partner might go to find the truth.

Scully is concerned for Mulder's well-being when he is the only suspect in a brutal double murder. Mulder can't remember the event. He remembers only voices and happenings that echo down a corridor decades-long. The memories seem to link his parents to the Cigarette-Smoking Man. Scully clears him of the killings fairly quickly, and viewers are allowed to get down to more important concerns.

Scully insists that Mulder's visions might not be true memories, bringing the show back into its deliciously wonderful vagueness. She discovers that he's allowed himself to be treated by an unscrupulous psychiatrist who used a powerfully hallucinogenic drug on him. She asks him why he would do such a thing.

Well, he did it because this is a Mulder-runs-amuck episode. While he's chasing his past, Scully tries to protect him from himself. Naturally, he ignores her advice. The plot is reminiscent of season three's next-to-last episode, in which Scully is manipulated by TV signals and she goes on a crazy warpath.

Nonetheless, it showcases Scully's strength and proves she can carry an episode, as Mulder is allowed to do so often. And for once, she isn't wrong; her analysis of the situation is dead-on from the beginning.

When Mulder disappears, Scully takes charge, even yanking the slimy shrink off his seat and hissing, "Where is he!"

When she finds her partner, he's nearing the end of his rope. He points his gun at her. "Are you going to shoot me, Mulder?" He turns to fire away from her. Clearly, she's the only thing keeping him grounded. (But this scene was too disappointing and recycled to be moving.)

Scully writes at the end of "Demons," "I fear agent Mulder may be pushed ever forward in impossible pursuit." The question left for viewers is, Will she feel that he needs to be stopped for his own good?

Plot problems: When Scully drives Mulder to his mother's house, and he drives away without her, how does he get the keys to the car?

Also, the mystery of how, after being wakened from a deep sleep, she arrives at his side in less than two hours when he is in another state, is probably a case for an X-file itself.

Also, the double murders—how, why, who?

Best scenes: When Scully flings open the shower curtain on Mulder. And at the end of the episode, when she leans like a protective mother to cover his crouching back.

"Demons" shows Scully's strength and loyalty toward Mulder. And more important, her ability to deal with him.

Gethsemane

Scully narrates the events of the season four finale. In them, she is forced to confront her own mortality while Mulder discovers the ultimate proof of extraterrestrial life.

Mulder is shown what seems to be a bona fide ET, yet Scully, whose cancer is killing her, is told that the entire X-files cabinet is full of lies. Worse, she's told that Mulder is to blame for her cancer. She informs him of as much—that he's dedicated his prime years to "the biggest of lies." As in other episodes, he turns his back on her and walks away. But the episode ends with him apparently dead of suicide.

And yet . . . in the scene in which Scully identifies the body of her partner, she takes only seconds to verify his death, and although she may not be the most fervent of characters, she shows no emotion at all. Viewers, by the way, are not given a shot of the body. Anyone could be in that bag.

Chris Carter evidently wants viewers to worry that Scully really would believe a comparative stranger's explanation of events rather than her longtime associate. She does seem to do exactly that—but just a little too easily, in fact, almost before the man can finish his sentences.

There's something amiss here, particularly in light of the show's newest tagline: Believe the Lie. Since Gillian Anderson and David Duchovny are filming a feature-length episode scheduled for release after yet another contracted year of programs, it's unlikely that Fox Mulder is really dead.

There's also the title of this episode, "Gethsemane," to consider. Can we expect Mulder to rise from his grave so that our Doubting Scully can believe?

Scully's brother is finally given a part in the series. Bill Scully, Jr., works for big brother in the military. He urges his sister to give up her X-files work and spend her last days in the bosom of her family. Frankly, he seems just a tad shifty-eyed. Is he who he is?

To look for: The writers of the episode are listed as unknown.

Some great, tense scenes between Scully and Mulder. And yet another great crying scene for David Duchovny (he does it so well). The alien/conspiracy thing is getting a bit tired, but it forms an excellent context in which to deal with the complex relationship of the lead characters. After four years of this dark and brooding exploration of

< S C U L L Y I S M >

Mulder, you may not be who you are.

paranoia, fear, deceit, and official culpability, Scully and Mulder have truly entered and become a part of that darkness. The brilliance of the series is that viewers have been made to care about these characters so much that they share the darkness with them.

But the Fox Is Out There, bet on it.

X-File Investigations

"Mulder, there is a
logical explanation for everything.
There has to be one for this."

Episodes listed by season number, show number, and title.

Alien abductions   1.1 "Pilot"; 1.4 "Conduit"; 2.5 "Duane Barry"; 2.6 "Ascension"; 3.9 "Nisei"; 3.10 "731"; 4.15 "Memento Mori"; 4.17 *Tempus Fugit*"; 4.18 "Max"; 4.23 "Demons"

Alien captives   1.17 "E.B.E"; 2.25 "Anasazi"

Alien cockroaches   3.12 "War of the Coprophages"

Alien colonization   1.14 "Genderbender"; 4.1 "Herrenvolk"

Alien DNA   1.24 "The Erlenmeyer Flask"; 2.10 "Red Museum"

Alien encounters   1.9 "Space"; 2.1 "Little Green Men"; 2.16 "Colony"; 2.17 "End Game"; 4.11 *El Mundo Gira*"; 4.18 "Max"

Alien enzymes   4.11 *El Mundo Gira*"

Alien-human genetic experiments   3.2 "Paper Clip"; 4.15 "Memento Mori"

Alien implants   2.5 "Duane Barry"; 2.6 "Ascension"; 3.1 "The Blessing Way"; 3.9 "Nisei"

Alien insemination   2.18 "Fearful Symmetry"

Ancient curses   3.18 *Teso Dos Bichos*"

Aquatic dinosaurs   3.21 "Avatar"

Astral projection   3.7 "The Walk"

Bees   2.16 "Colony"; 4.21 "Zero Sum"

Black holes   2.23 "Soft Light"

Black oil/cancer 3.15 "Piper Maru"; 3.16 "Apocrypha"; 4.9 "Tunguska"; 4.10 "Terma"

Cannibalism   1.5 "The Jersey Devil"; 2.24 "Our Town"; 3.6 "2Shy"

Incest   4.3 "Home"

Infanticide   4.3 "Home"

Killer fungus   4.11 *El Mundo Gira*"

Lobotomy   4.2 "*Unruhe*"

Lycanthropy   1.19 "Shapes"

Memory loss   4.23 "Demons"

Miracle healing   1.18 "Miracle Man"; 3.24 "*Talitha Cumi*"

Multiple personality disorder   4.5 "The Field Where I Died"

Mutants   1.3 "Squeeze " 1.21 "Tooms"; 2.2 "The Host"

Near-death experiences   1.15 "Lazarus"; 2.8 "One Breath"

Parasitic killers   1.8 "Ice"; 2.2 "The Host"

Pituitary gland theft   4.4 "Teliko"

Planetary alignment   3.13 "Syzygy"

Possession   1.15 "Lazarus"; 1.22 "Born Again"; 3.14 "Grotesque"; 4.6
    "Sanguinarium"

Prophetic dreams   4.8 "Paper Hearts"

Psychic bond of twins   1.23 "Roland"; 2.20 "Humbug"; 2.21 "The
    Calusari"

Psychic channeling   1.13 "Beyond the Sea"

Psychic link   3.8 "Oubliette"

Psychic photography   4.2 "*Unruhe*"

Pyrokinesis   1.12 "Fire"

Reincarnation   1.22 "Born Again"; 2.17 "End Game"; 3.5 "The List";
    4.5 "The Field Where I Died"

Repressed memories   4.23 "Demons"

Shapeshifting   1.19 "Shapes"; 4.20 "Small Potatoes"

Siamese twins   2.20 "Humbug"

Sleep deprivation   2.4 "Sleepless"

Stigmata   3.11 "Revelations"

Subliminal messages   2.3 "Blood"; 3.23 "Wetwired"

Succubus   3.21 "Avatar"

Telekinesis   3.13 "Syzygy"; 3.17 "Pusher"

Thought control   3.17 "Pusher"

Quick Facts

GILLIAN LEIGH ANDERSON

Birth date: August 9, 1968
Birth place: St. Mary's Hospital, Chicago, Illinois
Father: Edward Anderson, film producer
Mother: Rosemary Anderson, computer analyst
Siblings: Zoe Anderson; Aaron Anderson
Hair: ash blond, colored red
Eyes: blue
Height: five feet two inches
Education: elementary schools in London and in Grand Rapids, Michigan; City High School, Grand Rapids; Goodman School of Theater at DePaul University; National Theatre of Great Britain, Ithaca, New York
Degree: bachelor of fine arts in drama
Marital status: separated from Clyde Klotz
Children: Piper Maru Anderson
Pet: dog named Cleo
Credits: *Absent Friends; The Philanthropist; The Turning; Class of 96,* "The Accused"; *The X-Files*
Residence: West Vancouver, British Columbia, Canada

DANA KATHERINE SCULLY, M.D.

Birth date: February 23, 1964
Birth place: Chicago, Illinois
Father: Captain William Scully, United States Navy (died in December, 1993, of a massive coronary)
Mother: Margaret "Maggie" Scully
Siblings: elder brother, William Jr; elder sister, Melissa; younger brother Charles

Hair: red

Eyes: green

Height: five feet six inches

Distinguishing features: tattoo on back

Religion: Catholic

Personal habits: drinks coffee with cream, no sugar; wears a small crucifix

Nickname: Starbuck (called that by her father)

Education: University of Maryland's medical school; residency in forensic pathology

Degrees: bachelor of science; doctor of medicine; forensic pathologist

Thesis: "Einstein's Twin Paradox: A New Interpretation"

Foreign language: German

Marital status: single, never married

Best friend: Ellen

Godson: Trent

Lover: Jack Willis, while at Quantico

Federal Bureau of Investigation identification number: 2317-616

FBI badge number: JTT03316613

Early FBI career: joined FBI in 1990, trained at Quantico Academy; taught at Quantico Academy for two years

Current FBI career: special agent investigating X-files with partner Fox Mulder

Weapons: Smith and Wesson 1076, Bernadelli 7.65, Walther PPK, and Sig-Sauer P228

Abduction: October of 1994 by Duane Barry, traded to "Them" (aliens?), released January of 1995, ending in the intensive care unit of North Georgetown University Hospital

Result of abduction: unexplained aberration in DNA; metal implant in base of neck

Current address: 3170 West 53rd Road, #35, Annapolis, Maryland

Telephone numbers: home (202) 555-6431, cellular (202) 555-3564

E-mail: D_Scully@fbi.gov.

DAVID DUCHOVNY

Birth date: August 7, 1960

Birth place: New York City

Father: Amram "Ron" Ducovny (last name spelled differently from son David's), publicist and author

Mother: Margaret Duchovny, homemaker and teacher

Siblings: Laurie Duchovny; Daniel Duchovny

Hair: brown

Eyes: hazel

Height: six feet

Education: Collegiate Preparatory School, Manhattan; Princeton University; Yale University

Degrees: bachelor of arts in English literature, master of arts in English literature

Ph.D. dissertation: "Magic and Technology in Contemporary Poetry and Prose" (uncompleted)

Marital status: married to Téa Leoni

Interests: basketball, baseball, racquetball, power workouts, power yoga, writing poetry

Personal habits: mostly vegetarian

Pet: dog named Blue

Lovers: several, including Perry Reeves and Winona Ryder

Best friend: Jason Beghe, since ninth grade

Nickname: Hayseed, in high school

Credits: *Working Girl, New Year's Day, Twin Peaks, Bad Influence, Julia Has Two Lovers, Denial, Don't Tell Mom the Babysitter's Dead, The Rapture, Beethoven, The Baby Snatcher, Ruby, Chaplin, Red Shoe Diaries, Venice/Venice, Kalifornia, The X-Files,* commercials for Lowenbrau Beer and AT&T

FOX WILLIAM MULDER

Birth date: October 13, 1961

Birth place: Chilmark, Massachusetts

Father: William Mulder; divorced

Mother: name unknown
Sibling: Samantha Ann Mulder
Hair: brown
Eyes: hazel
Height: six feet
Nickname: Spooky (called that by skeptical coworkers)
Education: Oxford University
Degree: bachelor of arts in psychology
Marital status: single, never married
Federal Bureau of Investigation badge number: JTT047101111
Early FBI career: trained at Quantico Academy; joined the violent crimes unit under supervision of ASAC Reggie Purdue, was distinguished in pursuit of bank robber John Barnett
Current FBI career: special agent in charge of the X-files section
Former FBI partner: Jerry Lamana
Current address: Alexandria, Virginia
Telephone: (202) 555-9355

THE X-FILES
Pilot premier: Friday, September 10, 1993
Produced by: Twentieth Century in association with the Fox Broadcasting Company
Creator: Chris Carter
Executive Producer: Chris Charter
Co-Executive Producers: R. W. Goodwin (Canada), Howard Gordon (U.S.A.)
Producers: J. P. Finn, Rob Bowman, Kim Manners
Co-Producers: Vince Gilligan, Paul Rabwin, Frank Spotnitz
Directors: Chris Carter, R. W. Goodwin, David Nutter, Kim Manners, Rob Bowman, Jim Charleston, Tucker Gates
Director of Photography: Ron Stannet

X-PHILES

Definition: *X-Files* fans

Profile: typically male, 25–34 years old, college educated, residing in northeastern United States, considers self moderate television viewer but is also *Star Trek* fan, and an Internet user

The Secret Signs and Symbols of Gillian Anderson

Gillian Anderson was born August 9, 1968, in the northern hemisphere, during the summer (June 21–September 23), under the fixed fire sign of Leo.

THE SUMMERTIME PERSONALITY

Generally speaking, the summertime personality has more measured responses to life than those born in the other three seasons. Although they are enthusiastic, they are also more critical. Their energies are perhaps less focused on initiating ventures and more on bringing them to fruition. Summertime people tend to be a mixture of introvert and extrovert. Empathic urges to help and become involved with others are strong. Summertime people often experience an emotional interaction with people as well as with their work and surroundings.

THE LEO PERSONALITY

Leo represents the radiant creative energies of the individual, which illuminate the world around it. Ruled by the sun, the lion depicts fully realized expression via powerful and directed action. Leo energies can be service-oriented, discerning, and analytical.

Leos love to make their presence felt through grand gestures. They love to be admired, for their physical appearance and for what they do.

A Leo's home is her castle.

Female Leo notables include Mae West, Madonna, Annie Oakley, Myrna Loy, Lina Wertmüller, Mata Hari, Madame Helen Blavatsky, Rose Kennedy, and Amelia Earhart.

Leo's born between August 3 and August 10 need to adopt a heroic, protective, or nurturing stance. Assertiveness, honor, dignity, and faithfulness are qualities stressed here. They are proud of their strength and enjoy putting it to the test, usually in some constructive way. For the most part, they are extraordinarily faithful people. In their toughness, they are able to withstand many disappointments. However, they may need to watch their tempers.

THE AUGUST 9 PERSONALITY

August 9 is a birthday of psychological leverage. Those born on this day are a tower of strength to those dependent on them. They know what makes others tick; as students of human nature, they are not only masterful at sizing people up, they also know how to confront them, and when necessary, persuade them regarding what is best for everyone in a situation. They are not only good persuaders, able to win others to their side, but presume a great measure of accountability for those who come under their wing. They rarely give up or admit loss once they have embarked on a project. At times, however, they are capable of being callous to the needs of their loved ones, in that they may suppose they know what is right before hearing requests or suggestions. What they believe to be true for the welfare of others is not always correct.

As they are so often involved in group endeavors, August 9 people generally have structured lives conducive to regular, healthful habits.

Notables born on August 9 include Mary Decker Slaney, Ruth Sawyer, Lucille Ball, Isabel Allende, Melanie Griffith, and Patti Austin.

THE FIRE PERSONALITY

Fire is the combustive element. Fire can refer to acute feelings, and to their display. Fire is highly unstable. It must be kept carefully controlled to maximize its effectiveness.

Fire-sign symbols are dynamic and connote irresistible movement. The fixed fire sign, Leo, embodies the steady radiance of the Sun, its ruler.

The fire-sign person apprehends the world primarily via the intuition mode. Fire-sign people have a strong sense of themselves. Because of their impulsive disposition, fire-sign people are apt to have accidents.

ASTROLOGICAL INDICATIONS

Element: fire
Quality: fixed
Ruler: the Sun
Symbol: the Lion
Mode: intuition
Motto: "I create"
Dominant faculty: feeling
Image: balanced strength
Stones: yellow topaz (restores inner calm, eases stress), tiger's eye (grants vitality), ruby (strengthens heart energies), and milky yellow amber (grounds visions)
Colors: ocher, golden hues
Body areas: heart, back, spine
Musical keys: E-flat major and G-sharp minor
Musical compositions: Beethoven's *Eroica* Symphony, Sibelius's *Fifth Symphony*, Mozart's *Thirty-Ninth Symphony*, Mahler's *Symphony for a Thousand*, and Mussorgsky's "The Old Castle" from *Pictures at an Exhibition*
Plants: sunflowers, chamomile, lavender
Trees and shrubs: hazel, almond, apple
Attractions to: Scorpios, Capricorns, and other Leos
Medieval condition: hot
Medieval temperament: choleric
Medieval humour: yellow bile
Psychological orientation: subjective
Physical state: combustive
Strengths: structure, altruism, thoughtfulness
Weaknesses: righteousness, authoritarianism, tendency to prod

NUMEROLOGICAL INDICATIONS

Ruling number: 9
Ruling planet: Mars

TAROT INDICATIONS

The number 9 card of the Major Arcana is the Hermit, who walks carrying a lantern and a stick. The Hermit represents meditation, isolation, and silence.

Gillian Anderson Speaks in Washington, D.C.

On May 3, 1996, Gillian Anderson, star of Fox Television's *The X-Files*, addressed members of Congress, urging more education and funding for neurofibromatosis research projects.

Neurofibromatosis is a neurological disorder, and one of the most common genetic diseases of the nervous system. Gillian spoke at a luncheon sponsored by Neurofibromatosis, Inc., which provided the guests with the opportunity to learn more about NF.

Among those present were Senator Abraham, from Michigan; Senator Nancy Kassebaum, chairman of the Senate Labor and Human Resources Committee; Dr. Francis S. Collins, director of the National Institute of Health's National Center for Human Genome Research; and Dr. Martha Bridge Denckla, director of the developmental cognitive neurology division of the Kennedy-Krieger Institute in Baltimore.

Rosemary Anderson, Gillian's mother, also attended as copresident of the NF Support Group of West Michigan.

Gillian's poignant and compelling remarks were entered in the Congressional Record by Senator Abraham. (Congressional Record, pp. S5392-5394)

Gillian Anderson's Remarks Addressing Research for Neurofibromatosis at the Neurofibromatosis, Inc., Luncheon Held in Washington, D.C., Friday, May 3, 1996

Thank you. I am just listening to the very small list of my accomplishments. They seem so insignificant in the presence of such gurus as Dr. Collins and Senator Kassebaum. I'm very honored to be here. But I will say, this is much scarier than any X-file I've ever encountered.

I'm going to read what I have written. I may be able to look you in the eye, but at this point it's written down and hopefully I can make some sense.

My first lesson with neurofibromatosis came when I was sixteen, after we learned that my three-and-a-half-year-old brother Aaron had it. My mother took me to the first meeting of what was to become the Neuro Support Group of West Michigan.

I remember the social worker there talking to the forty or so people who had shown up. There were many who were too intimidated to speak, and there were many who were so excited about the prospect of communicating with people who for the first time understood what they had been going through, and also communicating the fears that they had experienced in their lives, that they couldn't stop talking.

I remember in particular one young mother who had just lost her six-year-old daughter to an NF brain tumor, and I remember a sixty-year-old woman who was trying somewhat heroically not to hide the many disfiguring tumors on her face. It was a very broad spectrum.

My mother tells me that some people never actually came back to that support group. I think for the many who remained over the past eleven and some years that the support group has been there, they have shared in the comfort of unbiased friends and fellow sufferers, and in the slow but gradual understanding of NF and its unpredictable complications.

I have watched my brother grow into a sturdy fifteen-year-old boy. We are among the most fortunate of NF families. My brother is mildly affected by it; so far so good. But as we learned here today, if we didn't already know, with NF, it is never over. He has a couple of visible tumors, skin tumors, right now. He may have no more; he many have so many more that they are uncountable. We don't know at this point. And then there's always the threat of the more serious tumors, which can come about at any time.

And I guess my one hope, regardless of what happens in the future for him is that the Joke-meister, as we call him, maintains his wonderful sense of humor throughout.

But is it not just Aaron and the West Michigan NF community. NF is worldwide, and it can happen in any family. And I must say that if the horror of this disease isn't enough to promote its financial support, something that has—that is just as important, and something you might want to consider as an added bonus—is that the study of NF and neuro research is already providing breakthroughs in understanding more about cancer. And we all know how to pronounce that.

I want to thank you for having me here, for joining me in an effort to raise awareness of a disease that is in dire need of acknowledgment, community education, and extensive research if we are going to find a cure.

Thank you very much.

Addresses for Admirers

FAN CLUBS
The Official X-Files Fan Club
Creation-XF
411 North Central Avenue, Suite 300
Glendale, CA 91203
($25 for a one-year membership)

The Original X-Files Fan Club
The X-Files Fan Club
P.O. Box 3138
Nashua, NH 03061-3138
($20 for a one-year membership)

BROADCAST COMPANIES
American Broadcasting Company (ABC)
Ted Harbert
Entertainment President
2040 Avenue of the Stars, 7th Floor
Century City, CA 90067

Canadian Broadcasting Company (CBC)
Visual Resource Centre
Nancy Staib
P.O. Box 500, Station A
Toronto, Ontario M5W 1E6
Canada

Columbia Broadcasting System (CBS)
Leslie Moonves
Entertainment President
7800 Beverly Boulevard
Los Angeles, CA 90036

The X-Files
c/o Fox Broadcasting Company
P.O. Box 900
Beverly Hills, CA 90213

Mail may be addressed to either Chris Carter, Executive Producer, or Jonathan Littman, Director of Current Programming. The Fox Network can also be e-mailed at foxnet@delphi.com.

FAN MAIL

Gillian Anderson (or David Duchovny)
c/o *The X-Files* Production Office
North Shore Studios
Building 10
110-555 Brooksbank Avenue
North Vancouver, B.C. V7J3S5
Canada

Gillian Anderson
c/o *The X-Files*
Building 75
10201 West Pico Boulevard
Los Angeles, CA 90036

Gillian Anderson
c/o *The X-Files*
1201 Fox Farm
Big Bear Lake, CA 92135

X-Talk: The XYZs of The X-Files

*"So what you're trying
to tell me, Mulder, is . . ."*

Abductee   Person who is or has been abducted by aliens

Apocrypha   Various writings either falsely attributed to biblical characters or kept out of the New Testament because not accepted as resulting from true revelation

Apology Is Policy   Tagline at the beginning of the show, beginning with "731"

Are you able to breathe?   Idiotic question asked by Scully in the pilot episode

Ascension   In Christian lore, the bodily ascent of Jesus into heaven

Avatar   Incarnation or embodiment of a god

Barry, Duane   Alien abductee who kidnaps Dana Scully and gives her up for abduction in his place

Believe the Lie   Tagline at the beginning of the fourth-season finale, "Gethsemane"

Beyond the Sea   Song that was playing when Captain Scully returned from sea to ask Maggie to marry him; played later during the scattering of his ashes

Black cancer   Amber fluid used to poison those infected with black worms, causing the person to die and the worms to emerge from the body

Black magic   Magic with an evil purpose; sorcery

Black worms   Extraterrestrial biological entities found in meteorites, emerging as an oily substance, then congealing into worms that can penetrate human skin and attach to the brain's pineal gland

Blessing Way   A Navajo religious ceremony

Blue Berets   Military personnel who "clean up" evidence of extra-terrestrial existence

Cancer Man   Mysterious cigarette-smoking man often present in Skinner's office; also called the Cigarette-Smoking Man

Chupacabra   The "Goatsucker" of Mexican folklore; a gray hairless creature, with a small body, large heard, and bulging black eyes

Church of the Red Museum   Vegetarian cult in Wisconsin

Cigarette-Smoking Man   Mysterious smoking man often present in Skinner's office; also called Cancer Man

Clyde Bruckman   Man who can foresee people's deaths; based on a colleague and friend of Buster Keaton

Coprophages   Dung-eaters

Crew-Cut Man   Has no official identity; Deep Throat's murderer; killed in "The Red Museum" episode

Cryogenics   Science dealing with the production of very low temperatures and their effects on matter

David Duchovny Estrogen Brigade   Female Internet fans of David Duchovny

Dead Horse   Remote Alaska town where Mulder searches for his sister

Deep Throat   A man in some highly-placed governmental position who first appears in the episode of the same name; he alternately helps and warns away Mulder in the FBI agent's investigations of the X-files; is murdered at the end of the first season by Men in Black

Die hand die verletzt   "The hand that wounds"

DNA   Deoxyribonucleic acid; nucleic acid bound in double helical chains; contains the genetic code of and transmits the hereditary pattern

Draw-string pants   Recurring fashion trend cited by Mulder as a reason he doesn't want to live forever

Endgame   Final stage of a game of chess, in which each player has only a few pieces left; Mulder plays an endgame when he has to choose between losing Scully and his cloned sister, Samantha

Enemies in High Places   People high up in the Washington, D.C., establishment who hinder or manipulate Mulder and Scully

E pur si muove   Italian meaning "And yet it moves"; refers to an eighteenth-century scientist's experiments with electricity and dead frogs

Erlenmeyer flask   Dictionary: a conical laboratory flask with a flat bottom and a short, straight neck. *X-Files:* container of alien DNA that Deep Throat died to protect

Excelsius Dei   Alzheimer's patient facility where ghost rape and odd pharmacological experiments take place

Exsanguinate   To render bloodless

Extraterrestrial Biological Entity (E.B.E.)   Living being originating off Earth

Extreme possibility   Paranormal or alien-driven event

Fetish   Object or activity to which one is unnaturally devoted, or which excites erotic feelings, as the Trinity murderers in "3"

Firewalker   Volcano-descending camera that films parasitic spores

Flukeman   Man-sized parasitic worm bred in Chernobyl's radioactive waste and brought to Newark, New Jersey in the sewage tanks of a Russian ship

Folkstone   Haitian-refugee camp run by a voodoo-practicing colonel

Fortean event   Unusual or highly infrequent meteorological phenomenon linked to alien encounters and cattle mutilations

Friends in High Places   Contacts in the Washington, D.C., establishment who protect Mulder and Scully

Gargoyle   Actually, a water spout; often in the shape of a "grotesque" creature

Gethsemane   Garden on the Mount of Olives; scene of agony, betrayal, and arrest of Jesus (Matthew 26:36)

Gillian Anderson Estrogen Brigade   Internet fans of Gillian Anderson, begun by, but not limited to, "women who love women"

Gillian Anderson Testosterone Brigade   Male Internet fans of Gillian Anderson

Golem   Human-like being created of the earth with *emet* inscribed on the back of the creature's hand; when the first letter *e* is erased, it crumbles back to dust

Go postal   To open gunfire on innocent people in a public place

Gray-Haired Man   Killer of X

Hall scene   In "Memento Mori," when Mulder embraces and kisses Scully on the forehead, moved by the knowledge that she's dying of cancer

He Is One   Message scrawled on the backs of teens injected with bovine growth hormones (or alien DNA?)

Herrenvolk   Master race

Hex   A sign or spell that brings bad luck

Humbug   Something made or done to cheat or deceive

IDDG   Intellectually Drop Dead Gorgeous; part of motto of the GATB

I Want to Believe   Poster in Mulder's office

Kill 'em all   Mayhem-inducing message sent by machines to people exposed to an LSD-like insecticide

Kindred   A gender-switching sect, possibly alien in origin

Krycek   Mulder's partner in Scully's absence; a double-agent

Lazarus   Biblical New Testament man raised from the dead by Jesus

Lobotomy   Surgical operation in which the frontal lobe of the brain is cut across; formerly used to permanently tranquilize violent mental patients

Lone Gunman   Magazine published by several conspiracy-obsessed men, including Frohike and Byers

Lone Gunmen   Name used for magazine editors above

Lost nine minutes   Mulder's recurring evidence of alien intervention

Lycanthropy   Magical power to transform into a wolf

Manitou   Algonquian name for a spirit that turns people into killer beasts

Man save man   Final signs of Sophie, the gorilla in "Fearful Symmetry"; she disappeared in a flash of light, turned up miles away, and died

Memento mori   Latin for "Remember the dead" or "Remember that you will die"

Men in Black   Super-secret government agents effective in hushing up, by any means necessary, things the government really doesn't want anyone to know

Missing link   Undiscovered intermediate form of animal in the evolution between apes and humans, such as the Jersey Devil

Mosquito-bite scene   Scene in pilot in which Scully discovers marks on her lower back that look like those found on people Mulder believes have been abducted; Scully goes to Mulder's motel room, drops her bathrobe, and asks him to examine the marks

MUFON   Network of women who have been abducted by aliens; all are dying of an undiagnosable ailment

Mulder, Samantha   Younger sister of Mulder, believed to be abducted by aliens

Mutation   Sudden variation in some inheritable characteristic, as the Chernobyl sewer fluke

Nystagmus   Involuntary rapid movement of the eyeball, as seen in psychic-photo killer Gerry Schnauz

Ouroboros   Greek meaning "tail-biter," a snake biting its own tail; ancient alchemical symbol of death and rebirth

Paper Clip   A secret operation that pardoned certain ex-Nazi scientists

Paranormal   Psychic or mental phenomena outside the range of the normal

Parasite   Organism that lives off another species of organism, usually while doing its host harm, as the unearthly worm in "Ice" and the Chernobyl fluke worm in "The Host"

Parent-Teacher Committee   Coven of witches in the episode "*Die Hand Die Verletzt*"

Past life   Life lived in another body prior to current life

Pentagram   Figure of five lines, used in witchcraft

Piper Maru   Name of an *X-Files* episode; a ship in the *X-Files* episode of the same name; name of Gillian Anderson's daughter.

Poltergeist   Ghost responsible for noisy and destructive disturbances

Psychic photography Paranormal ability to create images on film with the mind

Psychic powers Powers beyond natural or physical processes

Psychokinesis Mental ability to move objects or project one's will

Pyrokinesis Mental ability to set objects afire

Rat Boy X-Philes' nickname for the evil Agent Krycek

Relationshipper (shipper) Program fan who desires to see Scully and Mulder become lovers

Roswell incident 1947 UFO crash; many believe an alien being was recovered in Roswell, New Mexico, by the U.S. government before all evidence was concealed

Sanguinarium A place of blood

Scully's rational explanation Scully's customary method of explaining away Mulder's hypotheses; often SREs are so far-fetched as to make Mulder's belief in Extreme Possibility all the more credible

Sentient Having perception and consciousness, as the sentient building in "Ghost in the Machine"

SETI Search for extraterrestrial intelligence; network of huge dishes to detect radio signals from outer space

Skinner Hard-edged FBI administrator who reopened and oversees Scully and Mulder's work with the X-files

Speedo scene In "Duane Barry" episode, when Mulder emerges from a swimming pool in a skimpy red swimsuit

Spontaneous combustion Process of catching fire as a result of internally generated heat

Spooky Nickname given to Mulder by fellow FBI agents because of his interest in the paranormal and extraterrestrial

Spore Small reproductive seed or germ

Starbuck Nickname given to Scully by her father

Stigmata Bleeding wounds, resembling the crucifixion wounds of Jesus, appearing on some devout persons in a state of intense religious fervor

Stratego   Board game played by Mulder and his sister as children

SRSG   Last clue scrawled in blood by the murdered X

Succubus   Female evil spirit that descends on sleeping men to have sexual intercourse

Swastika   Best known as the symbol used by Nazi's, but in reality, a design of ancient origin used to bestow well-being

Syzygy   When a celestial body, usually the moon, is in conjunction with or in opposition to the sun

Talitha cumi   Means "little girl—arise," from the Bible (Mark 5:41)

Teliko   Evil West African folktale spirits who emerge at night to suck the life and color out of their victims

Tempus fugit   "Time flies"

Terma   Town in North Dakota; hiding place of a rock containing black oil/worms

The following is inspired by actual documented events   Words on the TV screen that kick off the pilot episode

The Truth Is Out There   Tagline from the first episode

Tooms   Eugene Tooms, a killer who can (1) stretch and elongate his body in order to squeeze it through small spaces, (2) tear out the livers of living victims with his bare hands, and (3) nest in a dormant state on the sustenance of five such livers for a period of thirty years

Trustno1   Secret password Mulder uses to protect his computer files

Trust No One   Last words of Deep Throat, delivered to Mulder after he's been shot down in cold blood by unknown Men in Black; also, words inscribed on the Cigarette-Smoking Man's lighter

Tunguska   Site in Siberia where, in 1908, a fireball crashed to earth, igniting a series of cataclysmic explosions; origin of rocks containing black worms

Unresolved sexual tension   Platonic relationship between Scully and Mulder

Unruhe   German for "unrest"

Voodoo   Primitive religion based on belief in sorcery and the power of charms

We are not who we are Warning videotaped by a scientist infected with an unearthly parasite found in the Arctic ice core

Well-Manicured Man Member of the Cigarette-Smoking Man's cabal; warns Scully she's marked for death just before Melissa Scully's murder

Wetwired Refers to mechanical circuitry added to the human brain

X Mulder's informant, replacing the dead Deep Throat; murdered by the Gray-Haired Man

X-files Unexplained FBI cases, opened originally by J. Edgar Hoover in 1946

Yatta yatta yatta Et cetera, and so forth; phrase first used by David Duchovny in an AT&T commercial; when used with a wink, can be the equivalent of "hubba hubba hubba"

Yellow rain Hot drenching of alien enzyme that acts as a catalyst to accelerate fungal growth

References

America Online: "X-Filer Wants Big Movies," October 24, 1996; "*X-Files* Star Exits Quickly After Wild Fans Get Pushy," October 25, 1996; "GameWorks Premier Party," MTV Arena, March 15, 1997; "The *X-Files* Forum," April 1997.

American Journal: April 1997.

The Anderson Files: The Unauthorized Biography of Gillian Anderson, by Marc Shapiro, Boulevard Books, 1997.

Associated Press: "I Want to Believe" (available on the "Gillian Anderson Web Site").

BC Woman: "Supernatural SuXXess," October 1995.

Discovery Online: The Learning Channel home page, 1997.

Dish Entertainment: "Hollywood Gossip," May 1997.

The Duchovny Files, by Paul Mitchell, ECW Press, 1996.

Entertainment Weekly: "Fall TV Preview," September 17, 1993; "X-Appeal," March 18, 1994.

Entertainment Weekly Online: "The *X-Files* Exposed," March 1994; April 1997.

Esquire: "Woman of the Year: Gillian Anderson," by Greg Williams, December 1996.

FHM: "Second Coming," by Anthony Noguera, 1996.

Flair Online: "Gillian Ascending," in What's Hip in the Movies, 1997.

Gannet News Service: "Gillian Anderson," 1997 (available on the Gillian Anderson Web Site).

"The Gillian Anderson Web Site!": April 1997.

Here Magazine: "Gillian Anderson: The Night I Said Yes to Mr. Wrong," by Tim Ewbank, August 1996.

The Late Show with David Letterman: Gillian Anderson interview, February 19, 1996.

Live with Regis and Kathie Lee Show: Gillian Anderson interview, May 18, 1995.

Los Angeles Daily News: "Salary Strife on *X-Files*," November 27, 1996.

References

Los Angeles Times: "Fans of *X-Files* Set Their Minds to Finding the Truth," January 11, 1996; "In Search of the X-Factor," by Jon Matsumoto, January 11, 1996; "Prime-Time TV Rankings," by Brian Lowry, January 11, 1996; "*Evita, Patient,* Win Top Golden Globes," by Brian Lowry and Claudia Puig, January 20, 1997.

MAX: "Gillian Anderson: X Symbol," by Henry Arnaud, July 1996.

Midday: "Anderson, Gillian," interview, CBC, April 13, 1995.

Movie Line: "Agent of Fortune," June 1995.

Museum of Television and Radio's 12th Television Festival, March 4, 1995.

Neurofibromatosis, Inc.: "Current Events," May 1996.

New York Times: by Frank Rich, February 24, 1991.

News of the World: "Gillian: The Disease That Threatens My Kid Brother," by Liz Jarvis and Leon Webster, September 1996.

Newsbytes News Network: "Review—Hellbender Game Combines Fury3 and Descent," February 14, 1997.

Parade: "Personality on Parade," by Walter Scott, March 16, 1997; "*X-Files* Star Joins Take Our Daughters Day," April 30, 1997.

People: April 18, 1994; "Occult Leader," by Tom Gliatto and Craig Tomashoff, March 13, 1995.

Producer: "XPloring the Paranormal," December 1994.

RealTime: Gillian Anderson interview with Leora Kornfeld, CBC, November, 1994; Gillian Anderson interview with Leora Kornfeld, CBC, September 16, 1995.

Rolling Stone (Australia): "Chris Carter, in 'The Virtue of Paranoia,'" and "The Princess of Paranoia," by David Lipsky, February 20, 1997.

Rolling Stone (USA): Gillian Anderson interview, February 20, 1997.

Rolling Stone Online: "Outtakes from the Gillian Anderson Interview," and "Trust No One," by David Lipsky, February, 1997.

Rolling Stone Rock and Roll Yearbook 1995 (Australia): 1995.

The Sacramento Bee: "Stars Usher in Modern Arcade," March 18, 1997.

Sci-Fi Entertainment: "The FX Are Out There," by Dr. Craig Reed, April 1997.

References

SFX: Gillian Anderson interview, July 1995.

Star: "*X-Files* Gillian Anderson's Wild Love Life," March 18, 1997.

Starlog: Gillian Anderson interview, April 1995; "Burbank *X-Files* Convention," by Stephen Walker, January 1996.

Sydney Morning Herald: "Gillian Anderson," January 1996.

TV Guide: "Gillian, Looks Like a Million," by Stephanie Mansfield, November 12, 1994.

The Unauthorized Guide to the X-Files, by Hal Schuster, Prima Publishing, 1997.

US: "Duchovny and Anderson," by Chris Mundy, May 1997.

US: "Secret Agent Man," May 1995.

USA Today: "*X-Files* New Mom Anderson Has No Time for X-haustion," 1994.

Variety: "*X-Files* Anderson Conspires on Movie Debut," February 13, 1997.

Washington Times: "Skepticism All an Act for *X-Files* Agent," January 6, 1994.

Wrapped in Plastic: "An Appointment with Dr. Scully," October 12, 1994.

The X Factor, by Chris Nickson, Avon Books, December 1996.

The X-Files Official Magazine: "With a Little Help from Her Friends," by Mo Ryan, Spring 1997.

Index

Index

Index

Index

Index

The Outer Limits Series

"There is nothing wrong with your television set.
Do not attempt to adjust the picture.
We are controlling transmission. . . ."

Both in its original 1960s form and as revived for the
1990s, *The Outer Limits*™ television series inspires critical
and popular acclaim. Now, in cooperation with MGM
Studios, Prima brings *The Outer Limits* into a new
dimension. Each volume features four short stories taken
from the old and new series. The novelizations are either
by the original writer or adapted by some of today's front-
rank science fiction and fantasy writers.

Volume One

• "Soldier" by Harlan Ellison • "It Crawled Out of the
Woodwork" by Diane Duane • "The Sixth Finger" by
John M. Ford • "If These Walls Could Talk" by Howard
V. Hendrix

ISBN 0-7615-0619-5 / paperback / 256 pages
U.S. $12.00 / Can. $16.95

Volume Two

• "The Choice" by Diane Duane • "Arena" by Fredric Brown • "The Message" by Richard A.
Lupoff • "A Feasibility Study" by Michael Marano

ISBN 0-7615-0620-9 / paperback / 304 pages
U.S. $12.00 / Can. $16.95

Volume Three

• "The Voyage Home" by Diane Duane • "The Forms of Things Unknown" by Richard A.
Lupoff • "I, Robot" by Eando Binder • "The Quality of Mercy" by Phoebe Reeves

ISBN 0-7615-0621-7 / paperback / 272 pages
U.S. $12.00 / Can. $16.95

The Unauthorized Guide to The X-Files

Hal Schuster

ISBN 0-7615-0845-7 / paperback / 240 pages
U.S. $16.00 / Can. $21.95

Whether you're part of the original *X-Files* cult or you've only recently tuned in, you'll get more out of the most talked-about show on television after you read this unauthorized, irreverent, no-holds-barred exposé. *The Unauthorized Guide to The X-Files* will help you:

- Deconstruct the grand mythological framework behind the mysterious plots

- Uncover real-life parallels to the program's dark intrigues

- Sort out the Syndicate—that anonymous clique that meets in stuffy drawing rooms

- Probe "The Project" the Syndicate is pursuing and find out who else—or what else—is involved

- Connect the dots in the puzzling relationship between Cigarette-Smoking Man and Mulder's own family

- Understand how a beach bum like Chris Carter could put together the spookiest show on television

- And much more!

Episode by episode, *The Unauthorized Guide to The X-Files* gives you the unvarnished truth—and puts it in perspective.

This book was not approved, prepared, or endorsed by any entity involved in creating or producing *The X-Files*.

To Order Books

Please send me the following items:

Quantity	Title	Unit Price	Total
_____	The Outer Limits, Volume One	$ 12.00	$ _____
_____	The Outer Limits, Volume Two	$ 12.00	$ _____
_____	The Outer Limits, Volume Three	$ 12.00	$ _____
_____	The Unauthorized Guide to the X-Files	$ 16.00	$ _____
_____	_____	$ _____	$ _____

*Shipping and Handling depend on Subtotal.

Subtotal	Shipping/Handling
$0.00–$14.99	$3.00
$15.00–$29.99	$4.00
$30.00–$49.99	$6.00
$50.00–$99.99	$10.00
$100.00–$199.99	$13.50
$200.00+	Call for Quote

Foreign and all Priority Request orders:
Call Order Entry department
for price quote at 916/632-4400

This chart represents the total retail price of books only
(before applicable discounts are taken).

Subtotal $ _____

Deduct 10% when ordering 3-5 books $ _____

7.25% Sales Tax (CA only) $ _____

8.25% Sales Tax (TN only) $ _____

5.0% Sales Tax (MD and IN only) $ _____

Shipping and Handling* $ _____

Total Order $ _____

By Telephone: With MC or Visa, call 800-632-8676 or 916-632-4400. Mon–Fri, 8:30-4:30.
WWW: http://www.primapublishing.com

By Internet E-mail: sales@primapub.com
By Mail: Just fill out the information below and send with your remittance to:

**Prima Publishing
P.O. Box 1260BK
Rocklin, CA 95677**

My name is _____

I live at _____

City_____ State _____ ZIP _____

MC/Visa#_____ Exp._____

Check/money order enclosed for $ _____ Payable to Prima Publishing

Daytime telephone _____

Signature _____